PLAYING WITH DRUM LOOPS

HOW TO WORK WITH DRUM LOOPS, SAMPLES, AND BACKING TRACKS

BY DONNY GRUENDLER

Audio Download Code 94639265
See p. 11 - Format: Length of Loop Audio

All Music Composed and Programmed by
Donny Gruendler

Acoustic Drums Recorded by
Chris Johnson and Christian Lundberg at Nuclear Records and Sound

Audio Mixing
Christian Lundberg and Donny Gruendler

Audio Mastering
Jody Whitesides at Dancing Deer Studios

Additional Metal Loops
Derek Jones

This book is dedicated to the memory of
Donald L. Gruendler Sr.

Pembroke Music Co.
A DIVISION OF CARL FISCHER, LLC
65 Bleecker Street, New York, NY 10012

DRM120

ISBN 0-8258-5982-4

TABLE OF CONTENTS

Part 1: Total Accompaniment

Chapter 1: Rock and Metal Loops

Chapter 2: Pop Rock Loops

Chapter 3: Hip Hop and R&B Loops

Part 2: Additional Loop Types

Chapter 4: Percussion Loops

Chapter 5: Instrument Loops

Chapter 6: Backing Tracks

Part 3: Appendices

CD TRACK LISTING (CD 1)

1. Introduction to Playing with Loops
2. Fundamental 1
3. Fundamental 2A
4. Fundamental 2B
5. Fundamental 3
6. Fundamental 4A
7. Fundamental 4B-1
8. Fundamental 4B-2
9. Fundamental 4C-1
10. Fundamental 4C-2
11. Total Accompaniment Loop Example 1
    Demonstration Track with Acoustic Drums
12. Total Accompaniment Loop Example 1
    Play Along Track
13. Total Accompaniment Loop Example 2
    Demonstration Track with Acoustic Drums
14. Total Accompaniment Loop Example 2
    Play Along Track
15. Rock & Metal Loop 1
16. Rock & Metal Loop 2
17. Rock & Metal Loop 3
18. Rock & Metal Loop 4
19. Rock & Metal Loop 5
20. Rock & Metal Loop 6
21. Rock & Metal Loop 7
22. Rock & Metal Loop 8
23. Rock & Metal Loop 9
24. Rock & Metal Loops:
    One Bar Combination Solo
25. Rock & Metal Loop 1a
26. Rock & Metal Loop 2a
27. Rock & Metal Loop 3a
28. Rock & Metal Loop 4a
29. Rock & Metal Loop 5a
30. Rock & Metal Loop 6a
31. Rock & Metal Loop 7a
32. Rock & Metal Loop 8a
33. Rock & Metal Loop 9a
34. Rock & Metal Loops:
    Two Bar Combination Solo
35. A Note on Swing Phrasing
36. Pop Rock Loop 1
37. Pop Rock Loop 2
38. Pop Rock Loop 1a
39. Pop Rock Loop 2a
40. Pop Rock Loop 3
41. Pop Rock Loop 4
42. Pop Rock Loop 3a
43. Pop Rock Loop 4a
44. Pop Rock Loop 5
45. Pop Rock Loop 6
46. Pop Rock Loop 5a
47. Pop Rock Loop 6a
48. Pop Rock Loop 7
49. Pop Rock Loop 8
50. Pop Rock Loop 7a
51. Pop Rock Loop 8a
52. Pop Rock Loop 9
53. Pop Rock Loop 10
54. Pop Rock Loop 9a
55. Pop Rock Loop 10a
56. Pop Rock Loop 11
57. Pop Rock Loop 12
58. Pop Rock Loop 11a
59. Pop Rock Loop 12a
60. Pop Rock Loop 13
61. Pop Rock Loop 14
62. Pop Rock Loop 13a
63. Pop Rock Loop 14a
64. Pop Rock Loop 15
65. Pop Rock Loop 16
66. Pop Rock Loop 15a
67. Pop Rock Loop 16a
68. Pop One Bar Combination Solo
69. Pop Two Bar Combination Solo
70. The Radio Treatment Practice Example
71. The Hip Hop Backbeat
72. Hip Hop Loop 1
73. Hip Hop Loop 2
74. Hip Hop Loop 3
75. Hip Hop Loop 4
76. Hip Hop Loop 5
77. Hip Hop Loop 6
78. Hip Hop Loop 7

CD TRACK LISTING (CD 2)

1. Hip Hop Loop 8
2. Hip Hop Loop 9
3. Hip Hop Loop 10
4. Hip Hop Loop 11
5. Hip Hop Loop 12
6. Hip Hop Loop 13
7. Hip Hop Loop 14
8. Hip Hop Loop 15
9. Hip Hop Loop 16
10. Hip Hop Loop 17
11. Hip Hop Loop 18
12. Hip Hop Loop 19
13. Hip Hop Loop 20
14. Hip Hop Loop 21
15. Hip Hop Loop 22
16. Drop Out Thought 2
17. Drop Out Demonstration Exercise 1
18. Drop Out Demonstration
    Practice Method 1
19. Fills Demonstration Exercise 4
20. Fills Demonstration Exercise 4
    with Fill Methods 1-4
21. Percussion Fundamentals 5-8
22. Important Note: The Tambourine and
    Shaker Amendment
23. Percussion Loop 1
24. Percussion Loop 2
25. Percussion Loop 3
26. Percussion Loop 4
27. Percussion Loop 5
28. Percussion Loop 6
29. Percussion Loop 7
30. Percussion Loop 8
31. Percussion Loop 9
32. Percussion Loop 10
33. Total Accompaniment Reminder:
    Play within the Feel of the Instrument Loop
    (Demonstration)
34. Rock & Metal Inst. Loop 1
35. Rock & Metal Inst. Loop 2
36. Rock & Metal Inst. Loop 3
37. Rock & Metal Inst. Loop 4
38. Pop Rock Inst. Loop 1
39. Pop Rock Inst. Loop 2
40. Pop Rock Inst. Loop 3
41. Pop Rock Inst. Loop 4
42. Pop Rock Inst. Loop 5
43. Pop Rock Inst. Loop 6
44. Pop Rock Inst. Loop 7
45. Hip Hop Inst. Loop 1
46. Hip Hop Inst. Loop 2
47. Hip Hop Inst. Loop 3
48. Hip Hop Inst. Loop 4
49. Hip Hop Inst. Loop 5
50. FX Loop Practice Track
51. Rock & Metal Backing Track 1
52. Rock & Metal Backing Track 2
53. Rock & Metal Backing Track 3
54. Pop Rock Backing Track 1
55. Pop Rock Backing Track 2
56. Pop Rock Backing Track 3
57. Hip Hop Backing Track 1
58. Hip Hop Backing Track 2
59. Hip Hop Backing Track 3

FOREWORD

Many students and younger musicians ask me how I became interested in performing with loops, backing tracks, and drum programming. This is the story that I share with them.

Versatility

Early on in my development I believed what all my mentors (and instructors) had told me: "If you are versatile, you'll always find work." As a result I worked on Swing tunes, shed my Bossa Nova groove, and whipped out the metronome to get my time together. I even brought a pair of brushes for a ballad in jazz band class! *I was going to be versatile and become a gigging musician one day.* Thus, I went through my high school and college years focusing on these broad musical styles. *Versatility was the key to my success.*

As I graduated from college and grew into a professional musician, I assumed (because of these formative years) that I was versatile enough to handle any playing (or recording) situation that was thrown my way. I went on quite a few years thinking this way! However, this abruptly changed with one phone call and subsequent job offer.

A Brand New Day

It was approximately 10 a.m. and my day in Los Angeles was starting as it had most days before; a little coffee, checking some email and then off to the day's most important activity: practice for my upcoming gig that evening. Then it happened: "Ring, Ring, Ring"—the phone rang just before I could go into my practice space. No worries, as I thought this would only briefly delay my routine.

It was a band leader in the Los Angeles area that I had respected for quite some time; however, I had never worked with him before. He went on to explain that he had a new CD coming out and that it was quite different from his previous works. This new CD was heavily based in electronics and subsequently the live shows would have to replicate the sound of the CD to a tee. He then asked me a very unfamiliar and intimidating question: "If I were to hire you as my drummer, can you help me replicate and integrate the various loops, samples and sound effects into my live shows?"

As I searched for the answer, my heart pounded ferociously. I then thought to myself: *No Way!* I have *zero* knowledge of anything related to MIDI or technology. Nevertheless, I want the gig. As these thoughts raced through my mind, I did what any working musician would do: I hastily answered, "Of course I can do that for your live shows. It would be my pleasure."

He replied: "That's great! I will send you a CD. As soon as you give it a listen, let me know. I'll schedule time to go into the studio to retrieve all the loops and samples that you'll need to program for the live show. Oh by the way, the tour starts in six weeks!"

We then said our goodbye's and hung up the phone. After a brief moment of being ecstatic that I was hired for the gig, I soon realized that "the tour starts in six weeks!" What was I going to do? I panicked! This uneasiness went on for the better part of an hour.

As I calmed down, I soon remembered that I had a friend in Detroit that did this type of work on a nightly basis, so I picked up the phone and called him. As I explained the scenario to him (and he subsequently gave me a hard time about accepting the gig), he began to describe some MIDI concepts and a few pieces of gear that I would need. I frantically took notes on any piece of scrap paper I could find!

Over the next week, my friend helped me get up to speed on many electronic concepts. We spoke every day and I ran my various questions by him and he guided me along the correct paths to electronic enlightenment. I then purchased my gear, read the manuals cover to cover, drank way too much coffee and had more than my fair share of late nights.

As I progressed through this crash course, I ultimately finished my programming before the tour began. As I took a brief sigh of relief, I realized that the most difficult part of the whole scenario was directly ahead of me! I now had to begin playing with these loops and textures! OUCH!

Uh Oh...Rehearsals

As I struggled through the rehearsals, not only was it difficult to play along with these elements, but I had to groove with them and a live band as well! It took a great deal of concentration and focus (which was tough to maintain throughout a ninety-minute show). Thus, I learned one extremely important lesson about my musicianship and drumming: I was not as versatile as I had previously thought. I may be able to play with a click in the studio and perform in a wide variety of styles; but I had a lot of growing to do in order to integrate, groove and blend with these modern loops and textures.

Over the course of the tour (and after each night's performance), grooving with the loops did become more comfortable. I now had a regimen: I recorded each night's show and on the bus ride to the next city, I took notes on how I could improve my performances and do a better job blending with each loop. I repeated this regimen nightly for over two years. Through this process I came to understand and master grooving (and blending) with loops. As I was perfecting this approach, the band had another CD and a few more tours.

As I moved from project to project, I soon found that I actually enjoyed the musical challenges (and subtleties) associated with programming and performing with loops. Consequently, I sought out artists that utilized these modern textures and began to work with them on a more frequent basis. In essence, it had become my passion. I was having the time of my life performing with singer songwriters, hard rock acts, pop acts, and even electronica acts (all of these situations used loops and backing tracks to augment their stage performances).

The New Versatility

As time passed, I became a specialist at working with loops and backing tracks. I also realized that prior to these working situations, I had ignored the trend of electronics in music altogether. Thus, I had also neglected an entire segment of work opportunities for myself! It was out of this thought that I also developed a passion for teaching these concepts as well. Thus, I did not want my negligent experiences to repeat themselves in the next generation of drummers. I went on to teach clinics and master classes that were based on my "tech" experiences and hopefully, I helped drummers in the collegiate system avoid falling into the same "versatility" pitfall that I had.

Current Teaching

I now preach that electronics and loops are just additional subjects that fall under the heading of versatility. These teachings also led me to become a faculty member at Musicians Institute (PIT) in Hollywood, California, where I created the curriculum for (and teach) two electronic-based classes entitled *Working with Drum Loops* and *Drum Programming and Loop Creation*.

In the end, it was the coffee-filled late nights, road notes and touring experiences that spawned many of the concepts in this book. I hope that you enjoy reading it as much as I enjoyed writing it!

Donny Gruendler

ACKNOWLEDGEMENTS

My Family and Friends

Thanks to my incredible wife Hope for her love, support and friendship; my mom for her unwavering support of my music; my gram for all of her support over the years; Chuck Silverman for his friendship, support, and countless hours of advice; Mr. Sandy Feldstein for believing in me, his time, guidance and willingness to help; John and Esther Good for their love, friendship and huge meals; Denny Freeman, Mark Goldberg and Mike Thompson for an amazing musical outlet (where I was allowed to grow); Rhett Frazier my musical brother-in-arms and confidant; Rick Holmstrom for allowing me to experiment with technology on a countless number of gigs; Ron Dziubila for putting up with me on those countless gigs; my groove brother Dale Jennings and the *Los Lobos Theory*; Danny Cox for all his advice and help; Derek Jones for his ears, advice and for always answering the phone to help; Robert "Jake" Jacobs for his sense of humor and advice; The Church of Monday Night Football; Steve Mugalian for tons of advice and for getting me to move to L.A.; Doug Deming for his friendship, shuffles and a million gigs; Darrin Klingman for putting up with me in college all those years; *Mr. Inspiration* Casey Scheuerell; Charles Chemery and Adam Conway from Julia Fly; Jody Whitesides; Chris Johnson; Christian Lundberg; The Percussion Staff at The Berklee College of Music; Tim Pederson for his support and especially encouraging me to create the loop-based classes at PIT. All my colleagues at PIT/Musicians Institute; Catherine Goldwyn and the staff at Sound Art; Mr. Jim Ruffner for all those lessons and patience; Mr. Joe Pastorio and Music Quarters for my first teaching job; Gloria Espinosa of Sasko's Drum Shop for her love and friendship; and everyone that has helped me grow over the years. Thank you so much for your inspiration, guidance and love.

The Fine Companies That Have Supported Me through the Years

Vic Firth Inc: Neil Larrivee, Mike Hoff and Rudy Gowern for believing in (and supporting) me for so many years; **Drum Workshop:** Mr. John Good and Garrison for the most gorgeous (and best sounding) drums I have ever played; **Paiste America Inc:** Rich Mangicaro for all his time, support and wonderfully articulate cymbals; **Remo Inc:** Michelle Jacoby and Bruce Jacoby for their support and friendship; **Alternate Mode:** Mario Decuitis; **Ddrum:** Mr. Kevin Packard; **Ableton:** Mr. Dave Hill and everyone at **Carl Fischer Music** for making this project a reality.

ABOUT THE AUTHOR

Donny Gruendler was born and raised in the diverse musical surroundings of Detroit, Michigan. As a result, Gruendler grew upalongside an unusually broad range of influences including Rock, Soul, Funk, Pop, Hip Hop, traditional Swing, Hard Bop, and Blues. It was during these developmental years that Donny came to love music *and consequently* wanted to become a professional musician.

At age twenty, Gruendler graduated from Berklee College of Music with a Bachelor's Degree of Music. At age twenty-one, he earned his Master's Degree of Music from Wayne State University in Detroit, Michigan. Soon thereafter, (while living in Detroit) Donny established himself as a first-call drummer for many of the local sessions, casino performances and tours.

Gruendler now living in Los Angeles, California, and can be found performing in a wide variety of musical genres. Gruendler has performed, programmed, toured and recorded behind such diverse artists as Kenny Burrell, John Medeski (of Martin, Medeski and Wood), D.J. Logic, Rick Holmstrom, iTunes first unsigned artist Jody Whitesides and numerous other independent Los Angeles-based artists. As a result, he has become an expert at performing with backing tracks, manually triggering samples, playing with loops and programming tracks (both live and in the studio).

Additionally, he has programmed (and played on) numerous jingles, created content for sample and loop libraries and has even written music for TV and film. Thus, he has extensive experience in these "tech" areas as well.

Gruendler is a faculty member at Musicians Institute (PIT) in Hollywood, California. As with his formative years, he believes that all students today should be well rounded and versatile enough to gain work in this ever-changing music industry. For this reason and in the interests of making drummers more "tech savvy," he has created the curriculum for two of the schools most popular classes (which he presently teaches): "Working with Drum Loops" and "Drum Programming and Loop Creation."

EXPLANATION

CD 1 

The most in-demand drummers have always focused on musical issues such as touch, tone, time, feel, and stylistic diversity. However, these techniques alone are no longer enough to insure success in the current musical climate. Many of today's biggest Rock, Pop, R&B and Hip Hop acts use loops, samples and backing tracks to augment their performances. Therefore, in order to stay working, many high-profile touring and studio drummers are no longer ignoring *the trend*: technology and its textures are here to stay. Rather than letting drum machines and laptops get all the gigs, today's drummers are embracing, working, and playing *with* them.

Drumming: On-the-Radio Training

From Eminem to Sheryl Crow, loops and programmed tracks are all over the airwaves. Many drummers need to realize that music on the radio is vital and as aspiring *working* musicians, it deserves our attention. Today (and tomorrow's) job requirements are present in today's Rock, Pop, R&B and Hip Hop radio hits. Therefore, grooving consistently with these loops (and genres) should be mastered. These new-found skill sets will not only expand your groove, broaden your feel and widen your sense of time, but they will also increase your odds of getting work as you develop from student into a seasoned pro. In addition, heaps of current radio hits will be tomorrow's standards and fair game on your future gigs!

With these realities in mind, this book is designed to be a comprehensive source for the aspiring twenty-first-century *working* drummer. It is an in-depth study of how to perform with drum loops, samples and programmed drum tracks within today's most popular radio styles: Metal, Rock, Pop, R&B and Hip Hop. Not only does this book include many drum loops, percussion loops, and instrument loops for you to play along with, but it also contains various combinations of all the loop types, and fully charted backing-track scenarios in each style as well. These exercises emulate the "real-world" performance conditions of the commercial drummer; they will prepare you for your future work as a professional musician.

Common Time

This book is written from a commercial, mainstream and popular viewpoint. Thus, the exercises presented within each chapter focus entirely on loops that are in $\frac{4}{4}$ (common) time. However, I do realize that popular music is written in other time signatures. But this study is already quite colossal, without worrying about addressing additional time signatures. Nevertheless, I may address supplementary time signatures in my future books.

One-and Two-Bar Phrases

Additionally, the Rock and Metal and Pop Loops will feature both one-and two-bar phrases, whereas the Hip Hop section will only feature one-bar phrases. Again, I do realize that some Hip Hop may feature two-bar phrases, but I am generalizing to a certain degree (for the sake of brevity.)

Format: Length of Loop Audio

Due to the CD space restrictions (700MB and eighty minutes of music), each loop example presented in this book is approximately one minute in length (except for the backing tracks, which are between two and four minutes in length). However, if you would like longer loop examples to practice with, you can download them free of charge from my website www.DonnyGruendler.com (click on *Working with Loops*). You will then be asked to provide the "Audio Download Code" listed on the title page of your book. Once you provide the code, you will be able to download zipped files of each chapter's audio loops.

Format: Order of Study

Unlike many other instructional books, the loop exercises presented in this book are not structured in order of difficulty; rather, they are organized into many different popular-music styles in sequential phrases, feels and metronome markings.

For example:
- **Drum Loops:** one-bar pop loops at 90 bpm and two-bar loops at 90 bpm.
- **Percussion Loops:** one-bar percussion loops at 80 bpm and eight-bar percussion combination loops at 95 bpm.
- **Instrument Loops:** multiple-bar Metal, Pop and Hip Hop Instrument loop phrases.
- **Backing Tracks** (which are made from all the previous loop chapters).

Due to this layout, you are encouraged to skip to many different exercises throughout the book and have fun, although I do recommend that you begin with a one-bar phrase before attempting its two-bar-phrase counterpart.

Basic Musical Assumptions

It is assumed that anyone reading this material has a basic knowledge of note values and rest values, including sixteenth notes and sixteenth-note triplets, and thirty-second notes, as well as drumset reading, basic chart reading and some level of coordinated independence. However, if you do need any additional information on basic drumset technique or reading, there are many fine books available that can aid you in your studies. Please look in Appendix G: "Supplemental Texts" of Part 3: Appendices (p. 95).

What If You Cannot Read Music?

I certainly suggest that you find a reputable drum instructor in your area and take some lessons to remedy the situation. However, I do realize that many of you that are reading this book do not have the resources to take lessons or do not have the time to attend those lessons. Therefore, you will have to intensify your conceptual and listening skills. This can be accomplished by studying "The Fundamental Four" (p. 15) and "The Fundamentals" 5-8 (p. 60) in their entirety. **Do not skip over these sections!** These concepts will expand and refine your listening capabilities, which you will need to complete this book.

More Than Drumming: The Reference Section

Just imagine this scenario: auditions are being held in your home town for the biggest Pop tour of the year. After it is all said and done, you and one other individual are being considered for the job. Both of you have great time and can groove perfectly with loops; but the other drummer can also run, program and maintain the MIDI/Digital Audio Workstation (while performing on stage). Thus, the tour manager does not have to hire an additional tech to handle this job. Who do you think will get hired for the tour?
Answer: the other guy.

For this reason, it is imperative that you also read through Part 3: Appendices (pp. 80-95) while you are working on the playing exercises. These sections will provide you with the basic knowledge needed to maneuver in this tech-savvy world and prevent you from losing the job in the previous paragraph!

This section includes a glossary of electronic-musical terms, descriptions of real-world working procedures and equipment setups, and tuning methods that will help you to blend with each type of loop. Remember, this information will enhance your drumming and musicianship, not detract from it. Performance knowledge and *reference knowledge* are the keys to success!

"Time" to Groove!

Alright, now that we have established that playing with and learning about machines is a must, it is time to implement these ideas and slowly build you're tech-savvy practice strategy. Don't be intimidated. It is important to realize that working with loops is very similar to playing with a metronome. It will be difficult at first; but with practice, grooving with these textures will become easier each day. Furthermore, loops can be more interesting and mentally stimulating because they also provide you with a number of musical subtleties to deal with, such as *feel, tone, and texture,* whereas a click only offers tempo information through a simple "beep". Here is a comforting thought: think of practicing with loops as if you're playing along to your favorite CD— education AND entertainment!

NOTATION KEY

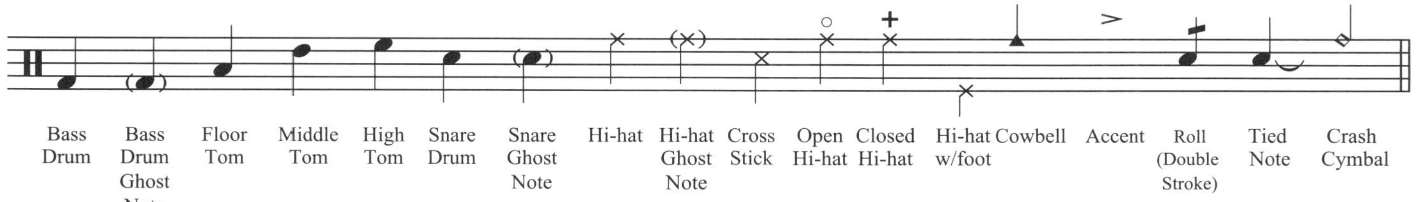

CHART READING KEY

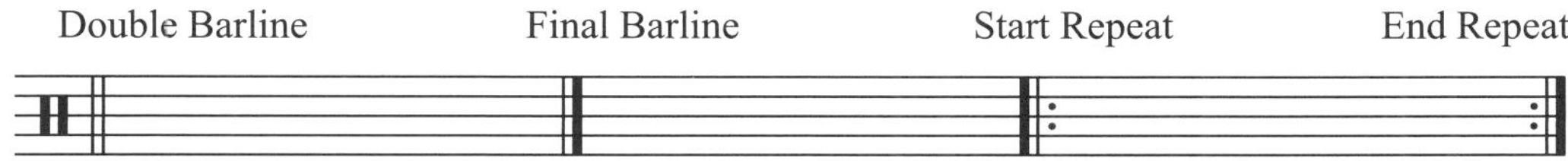

Double Barline: A double barline signifies the end of a section or musical phrase.
Final Barline: A final barline marks the end of a composition.
Start Repeat Sign/End Repeat Sign: Repeat signs indicate that a certain musical phrase will be repeated.

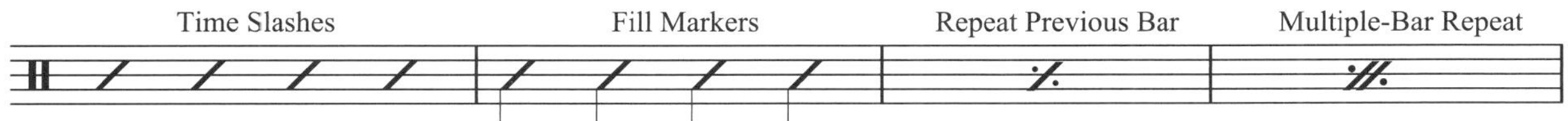

Time Slashes: Time slashes not only mark the beats of a measure, but they also indicate that a drummer plays "time" (i.e. grooves) as well.
Repeat Previous Bar: A sign indicating to repeat the previous measure.
Multiple Bar Repeat: A sign indicating that you must repeat a certain number of bars. There usually is a number above the symbol signifying the exact number of bars to be repeated.

Rehearsal Letters: These are symbols that are used to identify certain sections within a chart. In addition, each letter usually represents a new idea, groove and melodic motif.

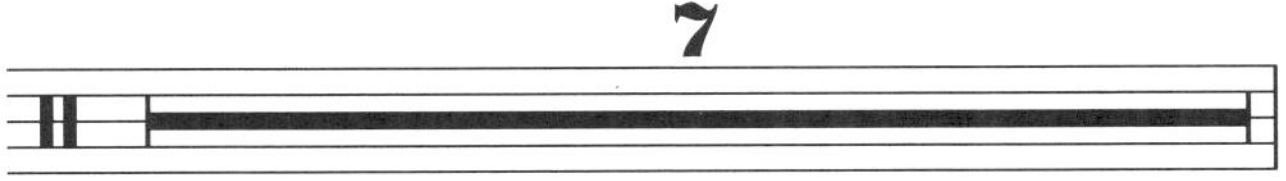

Multiple Bar Rest: This symbol indicates that you will rest for a specific number of bars.

D.C.

D.C. (da capo): Return to the beginning of the chart.

D.C. al Fine

Remember that D.C. signifies that you must return to the beginning of the chart. Fine is a musical term for end. Thus, you will return to the beginning of the chart (D.C.) and end when you see the term Fine.

$$\quarternote = 102$$

Tempo Marking: This symbol indicates that there are a certain number of beats per minute (bpm). In addition, this is usually related to a specific note value as well. So, the above example indicates that a quarter note equals 102 bpm.

Notation Insight

Furthermore, as you are reading through each loop example, please keep in mind that the notated (written) grooves are the basic hypotheses of what to play. It would be quite impossible to notate every little "sound" or synthetic texture within the looped groove. Therefore (just like chart reading), it is open to interpretation.

More than Drumming: It's Time to Talk about Music

It is extremely important that you do not think *drum-istically* when working through each chapter, concept or loop exercise. **This book is not only about drumming; it is also about music.** Musical sophistication, groove, feel, consistency, and comfort level take time to master. If you rush through the material and do not follow the proper methodologies—or read through the following section "The Fundamental Four"—you will be defeating the purpose of your study.

Intensified Focal Points

Drummers are the backbone of any great band. As experts in rhythm, we have the enviable position of exploiting our knowledge to color and shape the music. Just as your musical influences, drums, cymbals, and tuning help shape your *sound*, the use of loops will not only shape your sound, but the overall *band (or artist's) sound* as well. **Therefore, tempo, feel, momentum and note choice are extremely important AND INTENSIFIED focal points when playing with a group that utilizes loops.**

For that reason, I am presenting a comprehensive list of essential thoughts that you *must* examine every time you sit down to play with a loop. **Do not skip this section!** These essential issues are entitled "The Fundamental Four."

THE FUNDAMENTAL FOUR

Fundamental 1: A click track only provides one piece of information: tempo.

Working with a click track will help develop a steady sense of time. *However, turn on your metronome and listen to its vital beep. What information does your click track provide you?* Well, the answer is simple. A click track only provides one piece of information: tempo.

A click track is merely a timed reference point to where the middle of the beat resides within a given tempo marking.

It is merely letting you know that this is the exact tempo of 90 bpm. There is no additional information included within a click track.

Most drummers neglect to consider that a click track does *not* offer any additional (or helpful) information, such as play ahead of the beat, play behind the beat, play in the middle of the beat, play with energy, play a rock groove, play an Afro-Cuban groove or play a jazz groove.

Therefore, when you sit down to perform with a click track by itself, you can superimpose any of the previous feels and musical styles over the click and you will sound acceptable, as long as you play consistent time with the metronome. However, this same strategy will not work with loops because:

Fundamental 2: Loops provide tempo information and feel information.

Unlike a traditional click track, which is only a tempo reference point through a simple "beep," loops have many more musical subtleties to deal with, such as feel, beat placement and style. Therefore, not only should your *goal* be to play "in time" with the loop, but it should also be to blend *into* the loop as well. This will be accomplished by playing along with the loop while inserting the correct notes, the correct feel and the correct beat placement. Therefore, it is extremely important that you think in these broad musical concepts, rather than just a metronome marking and a succession of "drum-istic" coordination patterns.

Examining the Groove, Feel and Beat Placement of the Loop

Keep in mind that it is also quite possible to be playing "in time" with a loop and not line up (or groove) with it. Let's say that you will be playing with a loop that is 100 bpm and that is also placed behind the beat. Now let's also assume that everything you play with the loop is placed ahead of the beat. Here is the scoop: you will be officially "in time" with the loop (at 100 bpm), but you will not be grooving, blending well or playing correctly with it.

Fundamentals 2A and 2B

So in order to remedy this situation, let's take a look at the following two methods of loop analysis, Fundamentals 2A and 2B. Both of these systems will aid you in determining a loop's particular feel and beat placement.

FUNDAMENTAL 2A: DETERMINING THE FEEL OF A LOOP

Does it have a straight sixteenth-note feel or a Swing sixteenth-note triplet feel?

Take a listen to Rock and Metal Loop 1.

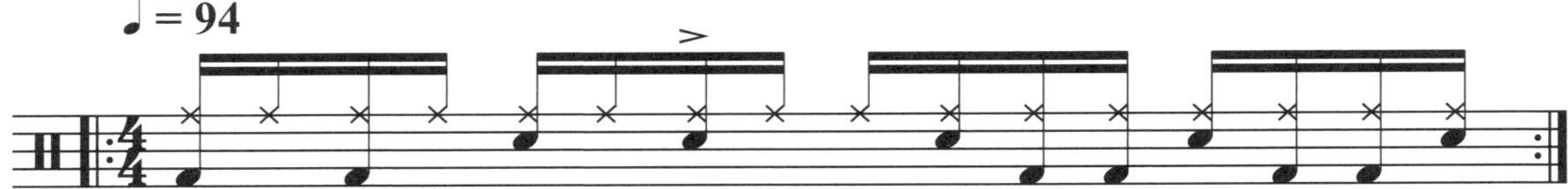

Now when you are listening to the loop, count sixteenth notes along with it.

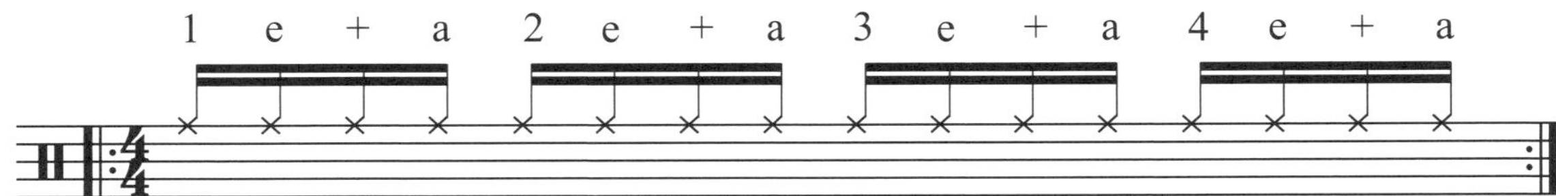

Does your vocal counting pattern line up with the loop? If so, the loop has a straight sixteenth-note feel. However, if you're counting sounds odd alongside the loop, try counting sixteenth-note triplets with the loop.

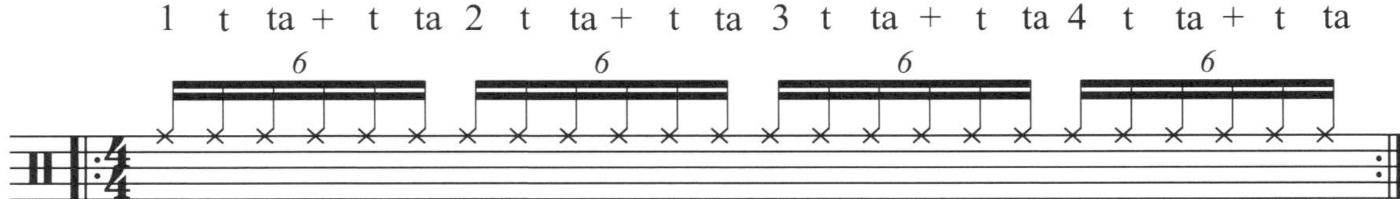

If this vocal pattern lines up, then the loop has a sixteenth-note Swing feel.

So, what is the overall feel of the loop? Does it have a straight sixteenth or a Swing sixteenth feel? Count along and figure it out! (If you answered straight feel, then you are correct!)

OK, we currently know that our loop has a straight feel. Now let's examine the loop's beat placement

FUNDAMENTAL 2B: BEAT PLACEMENT

Is the loop behind, in the middle or ahead of the beat?

To figure out the beat placement of Rock and Metal Loop 1, clap your hands along with the two-bar click track intro that precedes the loop and then continue clapping into the loop track itself.

For example:

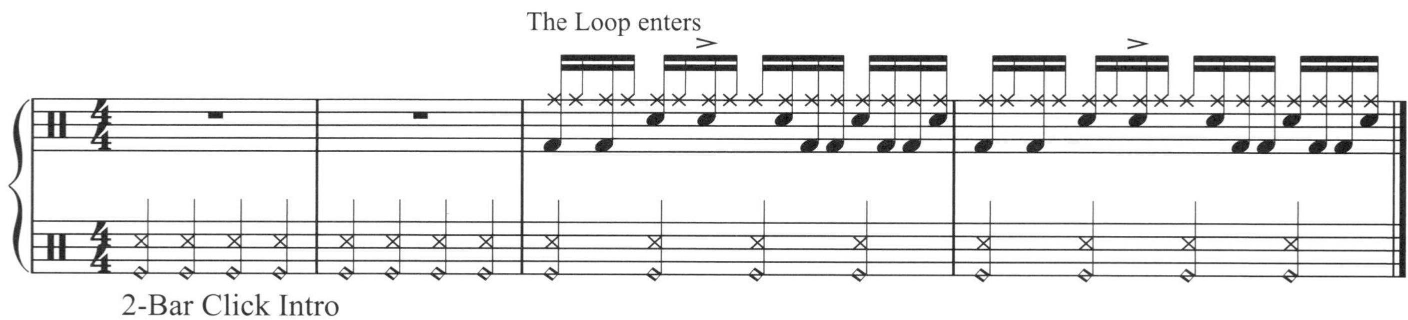

The X's indicate the click track and the diamond-shaped noteheads represent the clapping.

As you precisely clap with the click track in the two-bar intro (and then as your hands transition from that intro into the loop itself), try to notice if the loop is lining up:

- Exactly with your clapping (which would mean the loop was in the middle of the beat)?
- Slightly ahead of your clapping (which would mean the loop was on top of the beat)?
- Slightly behind your clapping (which would mean the loop was behind the beat)?

Repeat this step as many times as you need to in order to figure out the beat placement of the loop.

If these terms ahead, behind and in the middle of the beat are confusing, replace them with terms that you already know and feel comfortable with. For example:

- Ahead of the beat = edgy or anxious.
- In the middle of the beat = precise or dead on.
- Behind the beat = relaxed or lazy.

So what is the loops beat placement?
(If you answered "Ahead of the beat," then you are correct!)

After following these two steps, we have now determined that the loop has a straight sixteenth-note feel and that it is ahead or "on top" of the beat. So let's move on to our third step of analysis.

Fundamental 3: Do not disrupt the momentum of a loop

Listen to any radio hit that uses loops. What makes this track groove and flow as you are listening to it? Does is feel like a train that cannot be stopped? Is the rhythm so incessant and repetitive that it could groove for days without wavering in its consistency? Are you tapping your foot without even realizing it? If you answered "yes" to any of these questions, then you also realize the exact reason why many artists utilize loops in their compositions: loops add a relentless, repetitive and unwavering momentum to a track. As a result, you cannot disrupt that momentum, incessant rhythm, train, or foot tapping with inappropriate note values or busy fills that will detract from (or overshadow) the loop and its inherent drive.

Remember, *a loop is not a glorified metronome*. You must give the listener the impression that you and the loop are one *huge* groove. (Not two grooves: an acoustic drummer accompanying a loop). So in order to maintain that illusion, you must blend your fills and groove ideas with the overall repetitive flavor, feel and beat placement of the loop. This not only helps keep the loop/music flowing, but it also makes the drum part in a composition sound enormous!

CD 1 5 (CD1 17 PLAY ALONG)

So how do we do this? Let's examine **Rock and Metal Loop 3**. This example is also a one-bar straight sixteenth-note loop that is phrased on top of the beat.

Fill Choices
In the following example, I will experiment with four different fill choices while playing to Rock and Metal Loop 3. I will phrase my fills in the following manner: three bars of time and one bar of a fill.

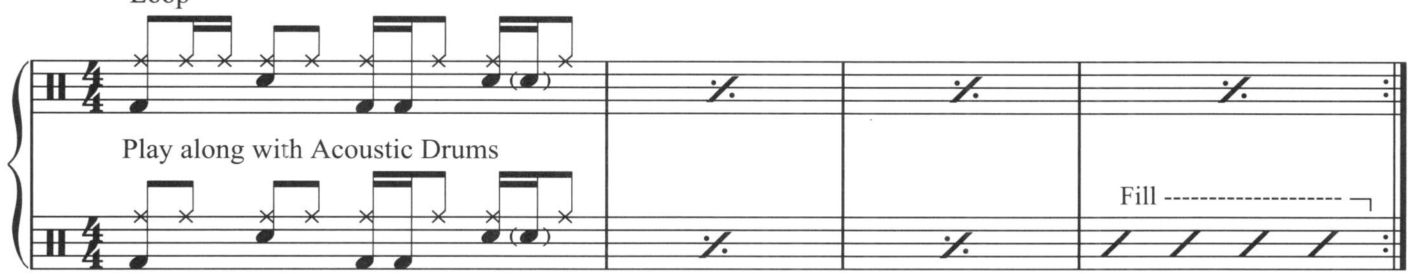

Examining My Fill Choices

Fill 1. So do you think it would be a wise choice to play a triplet-based (i.e. Swung) fill over this straight sixteenth-note loop?

Obviously this could not be a wise fill selection. A triplet-phrased fill would completely *grind* against the straight sixteenth-note structure of the loop and noticeably detract from its sound.

Inappropriate Beat Placement

Fill 2. In addition, do you think it would be a wise to execute a behind-the-beat fill (along with this loop example)?

Obviously, this would also not be a wise fill selection. A behind-the-beat fill would sound sloppy alongside our "on-top-of-the-beat" loop.

Backbeat

Fill 3. Moreover, the main focal point of this particular loop is its huge backbeat on beats 2 and 4. So it would also be inappropriate to play a long-winded fill that overshadows and does not include the backbeat.

When you listen to this audio example (although this is much better than the last triplet-based example), do you notice how this long fill covers up the overall groove? When the fill is played, the two instruments (loop and acoustic drums) aurally split apart from one another. Additionally, this choice would let the listener know that there are two drum parts going at once and consequently distract attention away from the cumulative groove. In the end it would destroy the repetitive and relentless nature of the music and the loops feel.

Correct interpretation

Fill 4. Now let's hear how the groove sounds when I actually play a backbeat within my fill.

Fundamental 4: Note choice: choose note values, tones, and tunings that blend well with the loop.

In addition to the previously mentioned relentless drive and unwavering momentum, artists also use loops to achieve *performance* and *sonic* functions that an acoustic drummer cannot. For instance, how many times do you hear a Loop on MTV that sounds like it is on an old transistor radio? How about a loop that sounds like it is being amplified in the depths of a cave? Furthermore, you can probably even turn on your local dance radio station and listen to programmed grooves that have flurries of bass-drum sixteenth-note figures that are so perfectly executed—they sound completely synthetic—as if to be from another planet. Thus, these types of loops have textural and inhuman performance qualities that cannot be reproduced on a single acoustic drum kit by a mere mortal! Therefore, it is also up to you to figure out how to preserve the loop's special qualities, while performing and blending with it.

Again, you should examine these note-choice issues before you sit down to play with a loop.

Fundamental 4A: Complement the loop and avoid "target practice."

Let's listen to **Hip Hop Loop 21.**

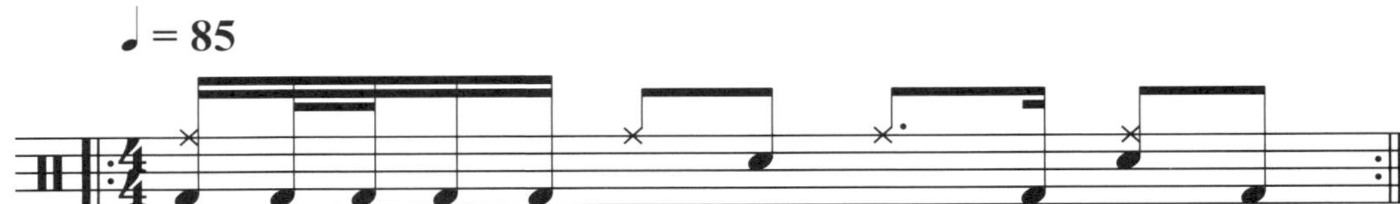

Upon listening, you will notice that this loop is playing tons of fast bass drum sixteenth notes on beat one. Therefore, you must avoid "targeting" (and playing) each one. Why? Not only may it be impossible to target (and line up with) the feel of every single bass-drum note throughout the loop, but by attempting to play every bass-drum note, it will also make the groove sound sloppy as well.

Here is the solution: **play fewer bass-drum notes.** By playing a few "choice" bass-drum notes, you will definitely be adding (rather than detracting) from the overall sound of the drum part. For example:

The first and last notes of a phrase are the "choice" (i.e., important) notes. Therefore, you must pick out the 1 and "ah" of beat 1's bass-drum part. This choice will reinforce the loop without interfering with it.

"When in doubt, leave it out."

Furthermore, let's imagine that you have a loop that has very few bass-drum notes. However, a couple of the bass-drum notes are in the middle of the beat and the remaining notes are ahead of the beat. Do you try to play each one with their exact beat placement (because there are so few of them)? The answer is *no, you do not.* Rather than playing each bass-drum note inaccurately, it would be best to leave out one of the difficultly placed notes and let the loop cover that note alone. Otherwise you will just sound sloppy playing along with the loop. My thought is, "When in doubt, leave it out".

Fundamental 4B: Choose tunings that help you blend with the Loop.

To illustrate this concept, I will tell you this story from my past.

I was on a jingle session a few years ago and I was performing along to a loop (rather than a click track.) I felt as if I was completely grooving and lining up with this particular loop. *I was sounding good.* It was a great feeling of pride, magic and ease, until the producer asked, "Can we try it again? I think you can get a little more dialed in with the loop on the next pass."

What? I thought he was *crazy*! I was *nailing* this groove. I immediately went into the control room to listen to the playback.

As the playback ran, I found that I was with the loop, but it was not *perfect* as I had previously thought. However, the acoustic drum track was completely within the feel, beat placement and flavor of the loop. As I listened in astonishment, I soon became frustrated. What about this track still felt odd? I kept listening to the playback for five long minutes and then "voilà!" the problem became very clear! I noticed that although my backbeat was lining up with the loop, it had a longer duration (i.e., Snare over-ring) than the loop's snare sound.

Let's listen to an example of my playing with **Loop Example 1.**

CD 1 ⑦ (CD1 ⑫ PLAY ALONG)

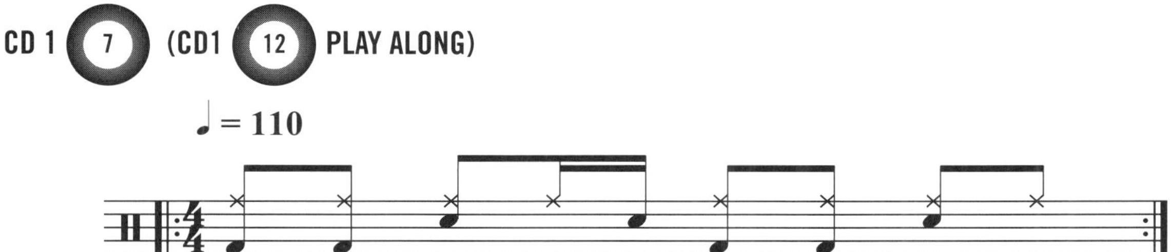

Notice how my snare has a wide-opening tuning and long decay time, which does not blend well with the short duration of the loop's snare sound.

I have notated both snares below with their proper durations.

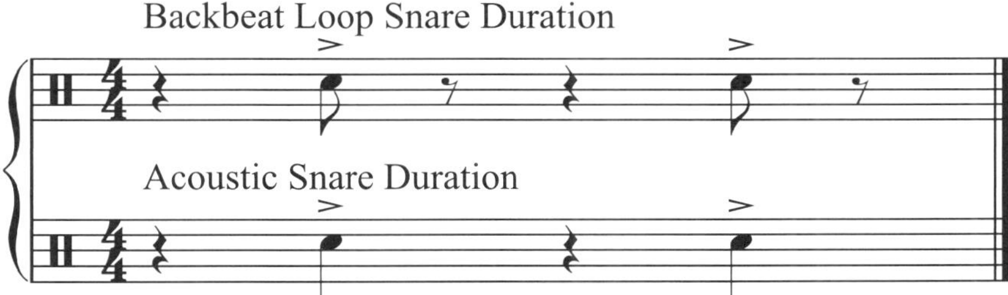

Remember to use your reading skills! An eighth note has a shorter duration than a quarter note. The acoustic snare (with the quarter-note duration) has a longer decay than the looped snare (with the eighth-note Duration). Therefore, the two snares are not lining up (or blending) with one another.

I ran back into the tracking room and immediately muffled my snare drum so that I could achieve a short and staccato sound, similar to the Loop. After I muffled my snare, it sounded like this:

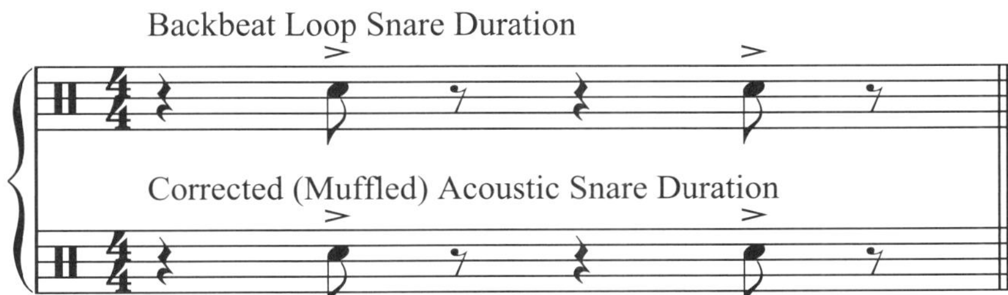

Now, the two snares are both ringing out as eighth-note durations and lining up with one another.

I then asked the producer for another shot at recording with the loop. I played exactly the same way I had in the previous few takes; but the last take was a keeper!

Here is the revised "Proper Duration and Tuning" example along with **Loop Example 1.**

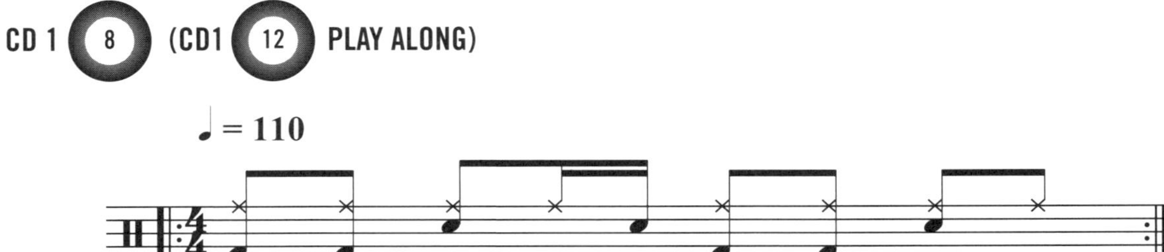

So how can you translate this story into useable information? If the snare present in the loop is dry and short, but your snare is wide open (with a long decay time), the two voices will not blend well together. Consequently, your snare tuning will give the listener the impression that you are not lining up (or grooving) with the loop. The groove will sound sloppy, even when you are executing it perfectly! Thus, even though you may be focused on playing appropriate fills, the correct feel, and the proper beat placement, you also must concentrate on the relationship between the durations of the drumset voices and of the loop's notes as well.

Fundamental 4C: Tones and Frequencies

Just as with target practice, you do not need to cover the same musical ground as the loop. Sometimes it will be your job to complement the loop *as you fit in and blend with it.* Please listen to another example along with **Loop Example 1.**

Instead of listening to the drum pattern, feel or beat placement of *this loop*, listen to the *sound* and *tone* of the loop.

What frequencies (i.e., pitches) are present in the loop? Obviously, this loop is *full* of high frequencies, but it lacks low end. Thus, it is your job to complement the loop with lower voices on the kit. Rather than playing the hi-hat with your right hand, you should play the floor tom to fill up the lower register. This will add a nice "bottom" that not only fattens up the loop, but complements the high ones in the loop as well. This will help the mix, groove and music sound larger than life.

One More Example

Let's listen to **Loop Example 2** and figure out what frequencies are present:

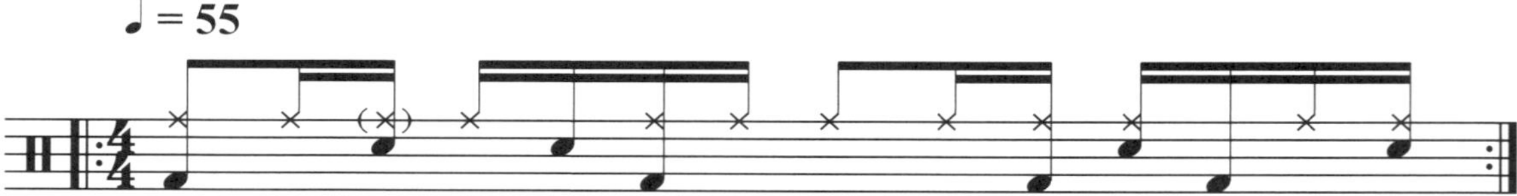

This time the loop has tons of low end, but it lacks a lot of high frequencies. Therefore, try to select higher voices on the kit, such as hi-hat, cymbals, rims and a tightly tuned snare drum. Again, you will be complementing the loop and making the whole groove sound gigantic!

Now What?

OK, we have now discussed some very broad and sophisticated musical concepts. These theories may seem very overwhelming at this point in your reading. They might even intimidate you from beginning to practice along with the book's loop examples.

So how do you get started? *How will you know what to play with each loop?* Well, think of "The Fundamental Four" as a starting point for each loop example. Therefore, each loop will constantly be a "Work in Progress" and ultimately, just like all musical concepts, they will not be fully mastered. Thus, rather than trying immediately to implement all four fundamental methodologies at once into your first loop, you must tackle a *single* loop from a very practical standpoint. Therefore, concentrate on *one Fundamental Four thought at a time, with one loop at a time.*

The Fundamental Four Outline

With this in mind, you should xerox the following page and place it along side whichever page you are working through in the book. Your ear will constantly be developing, and your analysis of each loop example may change over time as well. Just keep in mind that this is part of the growth process. Relax, groove and most importantly, have fun!

Fundamental Four Thought Outline
For Use with Each Loop Example

1. **A click only provides tempo**
2. **Loops have tempo and feel**
   a. Determine the feel of the loop by counting along with the loop. Is it straight or swung?
   b. Determine the beat placement of the loop by clapping along with the click intro and then into the loop track itself. Is the loop behind, in the middle or ahead of the beat?
3. **Keep the momentum.** Loops are used to add a relentless drive to the music. Do not distract the listener with inappropriate fills or note values. In addition, try to include the backbeat in your fills as well.
4. **Note Choice**
   a. **Complement the loop and avoid "target practice."** Do not instantly feel the need to play every note in the loop, especially if there are a lot of notes or a strange beat placement of those notes. Remember that playing all of them could sound sloppy. "When in doubt, leave it out."
   b. **Choose tunings that help you blend with the loop.** Try to match the duration (length) of your notes to the duration of the loop's notes, especially the backbeat. If you neglect this issue, it may still sound like you are not lining up with the loop.
   c. **Tones and Frequencies.** Listen to the sound and tone of the loop. What frequencies are present in the loop? If there are high frequencies, play low tones on the kit. If there are low frequencies, play high tones on the kit.

Part 1:
Total Accompaniment

The most common and frequent loop concept is "Total Accompaniment." This concept entails playing the exact drumset rhythm that is being performed by the drum loop. This technique is all over the radio; it not only fattens up the original loop, but it gives it a human element as well.

Here is an Example:

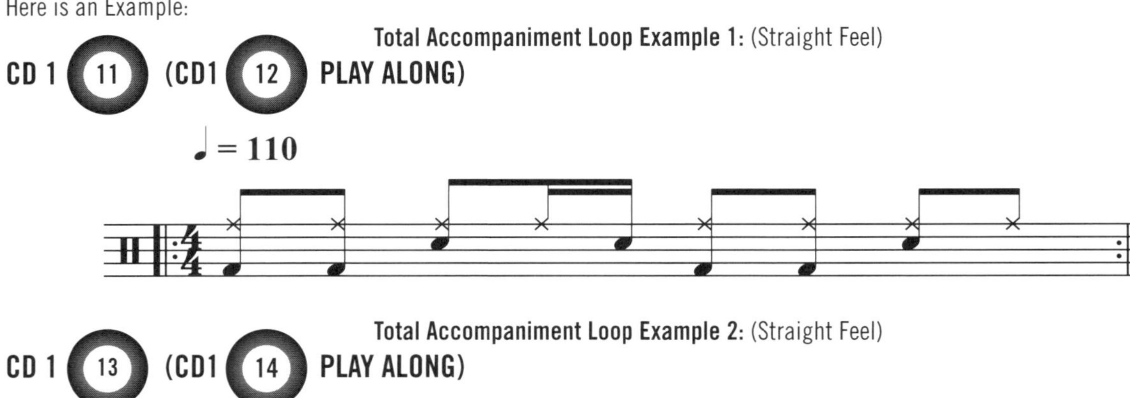

Total Accompaniment Loop Example 1: (Straight Feel)

CD 1 (11) (CD1 (12) **PLAY ALONG**)

Total Accompaniment Loop Example 2: (Straight Feel)

CD 1 (13) (CD1 (14) **PLAY ALONG**)

Notation Reminder – Ghost Note

**A Ghost Note is present on the hi-hat. A
Ghost Note is a note that is played softly, which is felt rather than heard.**

CD 1 (14)

Chapter 1: Rock and Metal Loops
94–130 bpm
Straight Eighth- and Sixteenth-Note Feels

During the past decade, many of the biggest Rock acts fused the most aggressive elements of Hip Hop and Heavy Metal into one cohesive sound. This style became (and still is) extremely popular by incorporating hip-hop beats and textures into an alternative Rock and Metal setting. This movement spawned many successful bands such as Korn, Limp BizKit and Linkin Park.

In this chapter, you will find many loops that represent this style. Section 1A deals with one-bar phrases and Section 1B with two-bar phrases.

As you listen to each loop, follow the clapping and analysis methods from Fundamental 2B: Beat Placement (p. 16). Then write in ahead, in the middle or behind the beat in the space provided. For example:

Beat Placement___________
(Answers are provided on p. 31)

Section 1A: One-Bar Phrases

Rock and Metal Loop 1　　　　　　　　**Beat Placement**___________

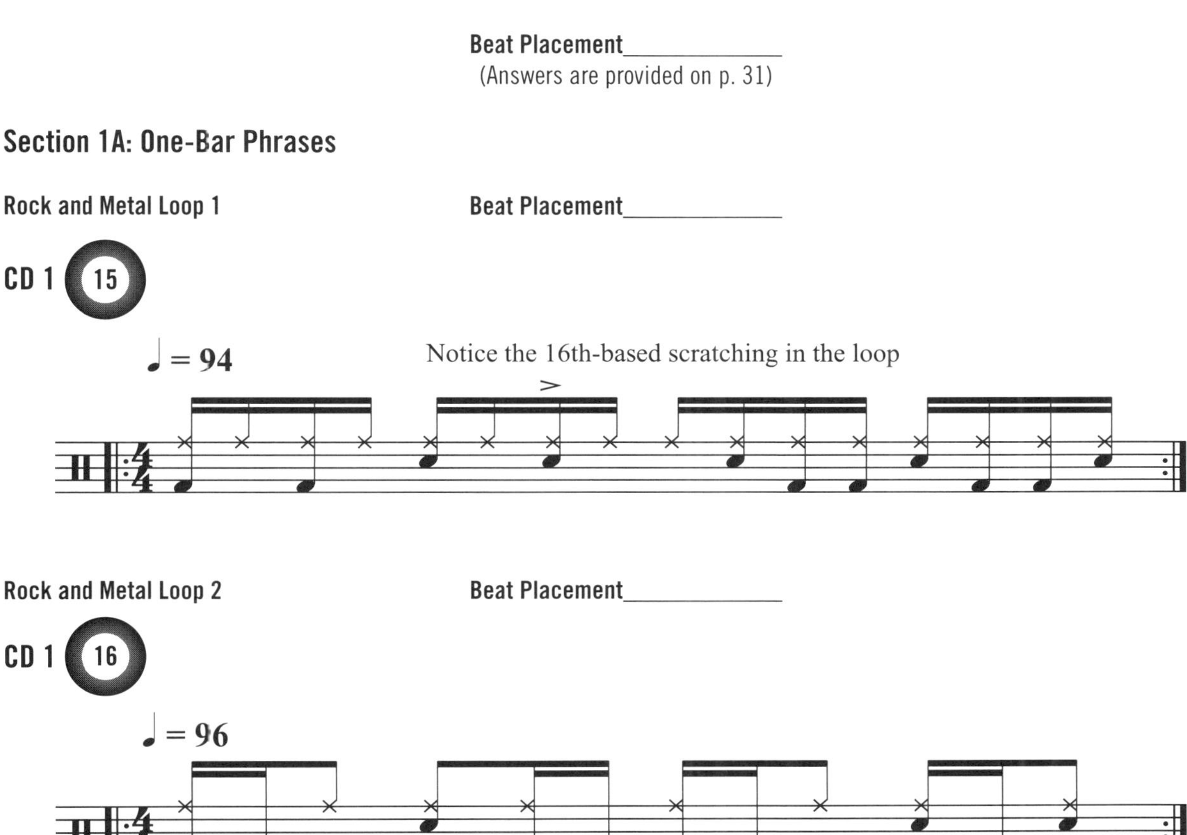

Rock and Metal Loop 2　　　　　　　　**Beat Placement**___________

Rock and Metal Loop 3   Beat Placement_____________

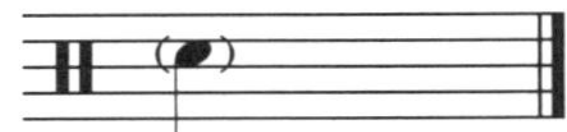

Notation Reminder – Ghost Note

In Rock and Metal Loop 3: a Ghost Note is present on the snare.
A Ghost Note is a note that is played softly, which is felt rather than heard.

CD 1   17

Rock and Metal Loop 4   Beat Placement_____________

Total Accompaniment Note Choice Reminder:
Play an appropriate hi-hat pattern with the bass drum and snare pattern notated below:

CD 1   18

Notice scratches with the main Kick and Snare Pattern

Rock and Metal Loop 5   Beat Placement_____________

CD 1   19

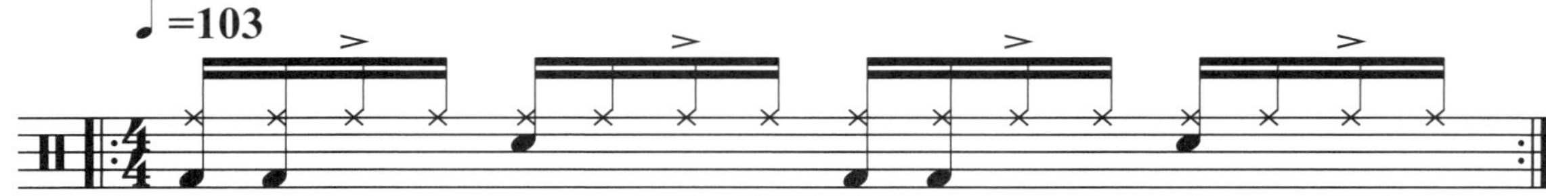

Rock and Metal Loop 6   Beat Placement_____________

CD 1   20

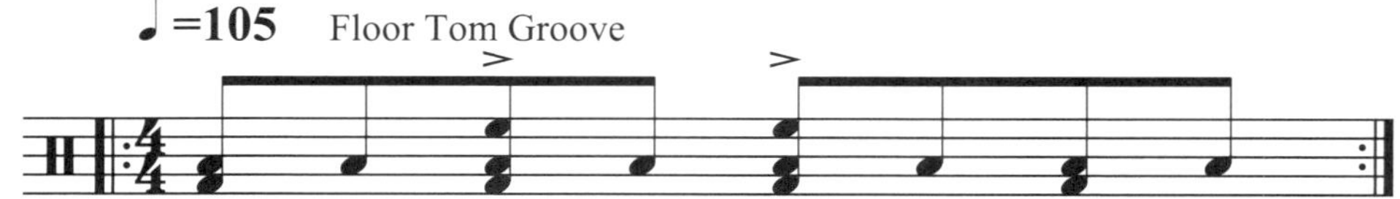

Total Accompaniment Reminder:
Play an appropriate hi-hat pattern with the bass drum and snare pattern notated below:

Notation Reminder – Tied Note

A tied note is present on the bass drum.
A tie connects the first note to the second notes duration; however, the second note is not played.

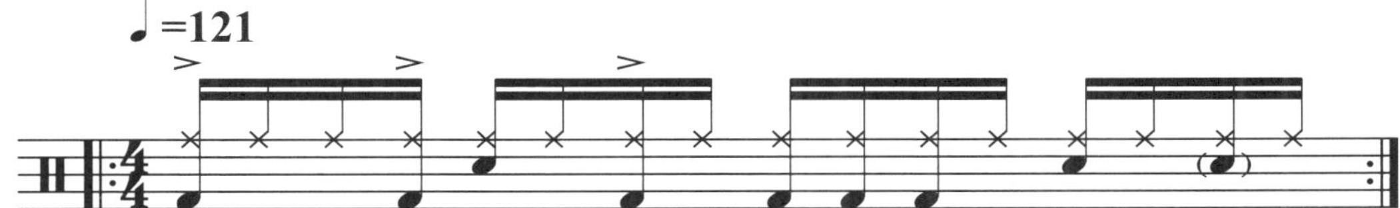

A Note on Combination Solos

On the following page there is a combination solo comprised of all the Rock and Metal loops from the previous section. By playing to all of the loops in a sequential order, you will learn how to "land on your feet" within each loop example's beat placement and character. Therefore, when you transition from one loop to the next in the solo, you will be forced to acclimate yourself to each different loop in each subsequent measure.

Rock and Metal Loops: One-Bar Combination Solo

Notation Reminder: Start Repeats and End Repeats (Repeat Signs)

As you read (and play) through this solo, please notice that each line (staff) of the solo has a repeat sign. Therefore, you will play each line twice.

CD 1 **24**

Section 1B: Two-Bar Phrases

Rock and Metal Loop 1a　　　　**Beat Placement___________**

Notation Reminder – Hi-hat Opening

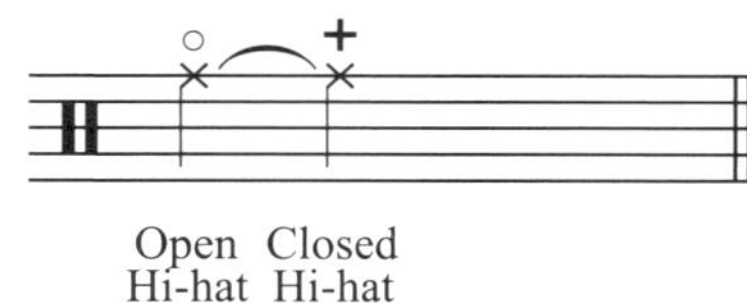

A Hi-hat opening is present on beat 1 of measure two.

CD 1 **25**

Rock and Metal Loop 2a Beat Placement________________

CD 1 (26)

♩ = 96

Rock and Metal Loop 3a

CD 1 (27)

♩ = 98

Rock and Metal Loop 4a Beat Placement________________

Total Accompaniment Note Choice Reminder:
Play an appropriate hi-hat pattern with the bass drum and snare pattern notated below:

CD 1 (28)

♩ =101

Rock and Metal Loop 5a Beat Placement________________

CD 1 (29)

♩ =103

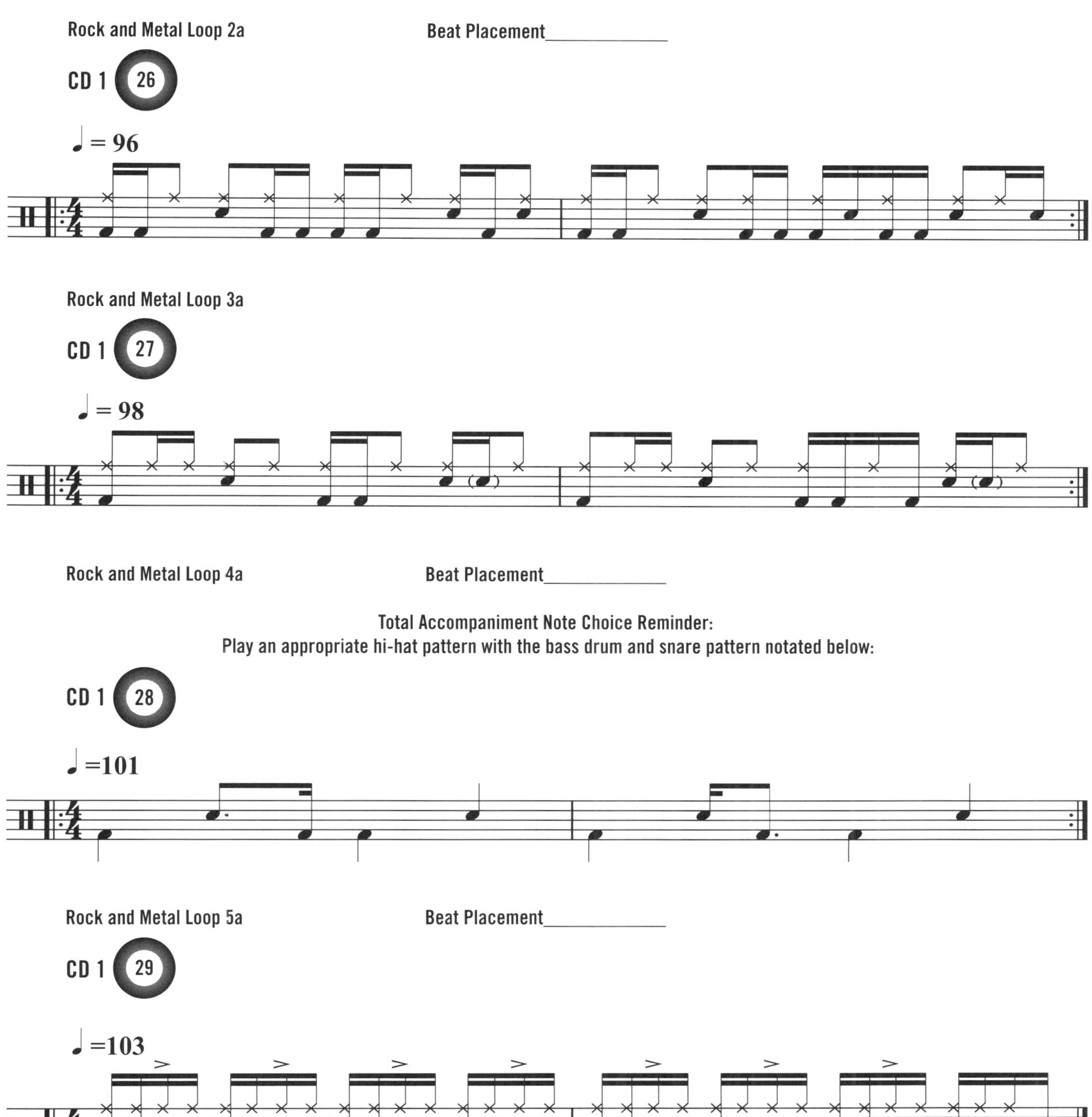

Rock and Metal Loop 6a   Beat Placement____________

Notation Key Reminder:
Notice that there is a High, Middle and Floor Tom notated for this Loop Example

CD 1 **30**

Rock and Metal Loop 7a   Beat Placement____________

Total Accompaniment Note Choice Reminder:
Play an appropriate Hi-hat pattern with the Bass Drum and Snare pattern Notated below:

CD 1 **31**

Rock and Metal Loop 8a   Beat Placement____________

CD 1 **32**

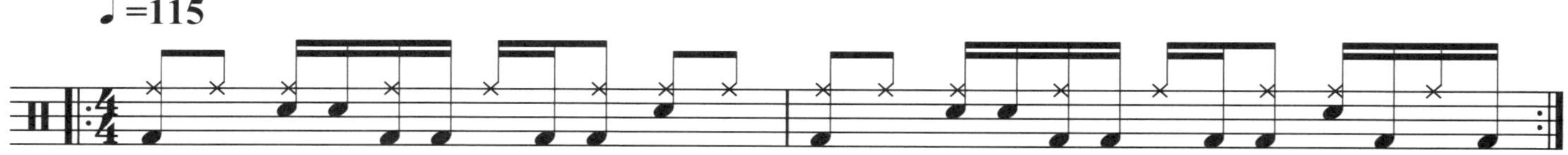

Rock and Metal Loop 9a   Beat Placement____________

CD 1 **33**

Two Bar Combination Solo

Notation Reminder: Start Repeats and End Repeats (Repeat Signs)
As you read (and play) through this solo, please notice that each line (stave) of the solo has a repeat sign.
Therefore, you will play each line twice.

Beat Placement Answers

Beat Placement Key
AH = Ahead of the Beat
Mid = Middle of the Beat
BH= Behind the Beat

One-Bar Phrases	Two-Bar Phrases
Rock and Metal Loop 1 = AH	Rock and Metal Loop 1a = AH
Rock and Metal Loop 2 = AH	Rock and Metal Loop 2a = AH
Rock and Metal Loop 3 = AH	Rock and Metal Loop 3a = AH
Rock and Metal Loop 4 = BH	Rock and Metal Loop 4a = BH
Rock and Metal Loop 5 = AH	Rock and Metal Loop 5a = AH
Rock and Metal Loop 6 = AH	Rock and Metal Loop 6a = AH
Rock and Metal Loop 7 = AH	Rock and Metal Loop 7a = AH
Rock and Metal Loop 8 = AH	Rock and Metal Loop 8a = AH
Rock and Metal Loop 9 = AH	Rock and Metal Loop 9a = AH

Stylistic consideration of beat placement: Most Rock and Metal grooves are______________of the beat.
Answer: Ahead (rarely is this style of music played in the middle of the beat).

Chapter 2: Pop Rock Loops
70–110 bpm
Straight and Swing Eighth- and Sixteenth-Note Feels

This form of Rock is catchy and energetic enough to appeal to younger listeners, but also mainstream enough to appeal to adults as well. It has huge chorus hooks, arena-Rock instrumentation, many layered loop textures and a definite backbeat. In addition, the production is clean, polished, and bright, making full use of the advances in recording and loop technology that had taken place during the 1980s and 1990s. Artists such as Michelle Branch, Avril Lavigne and Alanis Morissette exemplify the Pop Rock genre.

As you listen to each loop, follow the feel, counting, clapping and analysis methods from Fundamental 2A on p. 16. Then write in either straight or swing feel in the space provided. For example:

Feel_______________
(Answers are provided on p. 44)

Have fun!

A Note on Swing Phrasing

The majority of (but not all) contemporary Pop and Rock music is based on straight eighth- and sixteenth-note phrases. However, it can also be appropriate to "swing" your phrases to give the time feel a more loose or relaxed sensibility as well. In order to properly identify a swing in a phrase in the following chapters, follow the steps outlined below.

CD 1 35 **(CD1** 36 **PLAY ALONG)**

Demonstration:
1. Let's take a listen to **Pop Rock Loop 1**.

2. Now, just like Fundamental 2A, lets count straight sixteenths along with the loop:

Obviously, this pattern does not line up with the loop. Therefore, it is not a straight sixteenth-note-based loop.

3. Now, try counting sixteenth-note triplets with the loop:

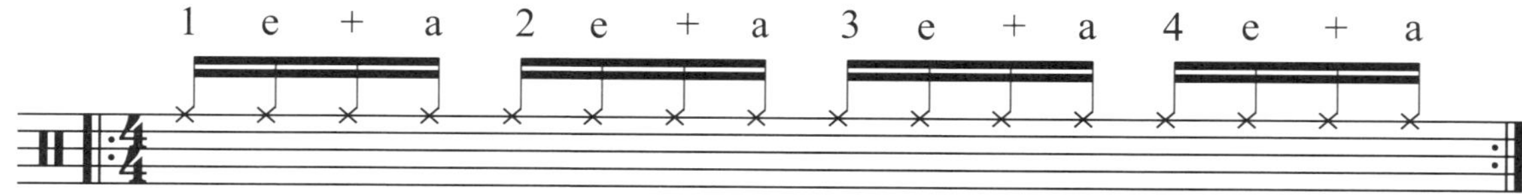

Ah ha! This vocal pattern lines up! This indicates that the loop has a sixteenth-note swing feel.

And although the loop is notated as a straight sixteenth-note groove, the loop is actually being performed as sixteenth-note triplets. For example:

To sum up this concept:
If you see straight sixteenth-notes like these:

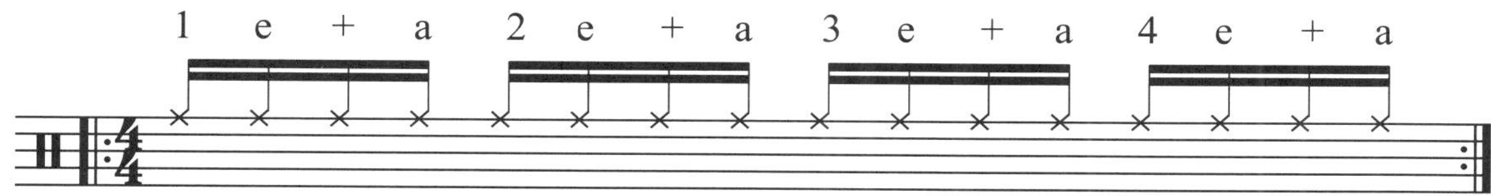

you may need to interpret them as and phrase them like sixteenth-note triplets.

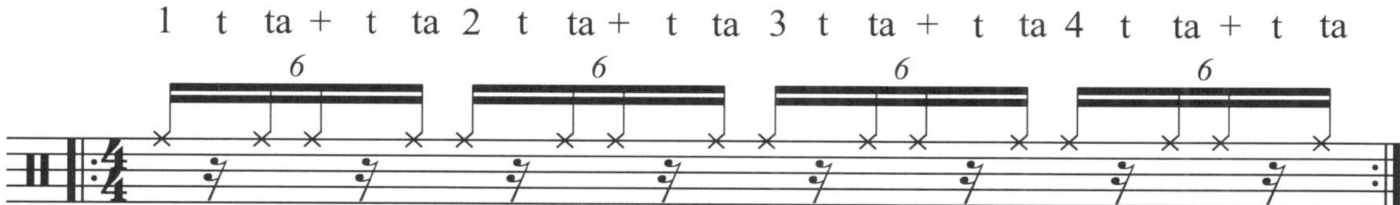

Try to count the sixteenth-note triplets as "swing sixteenth notes."

Phrasing of Swing-16th Counting (within a Triplet Feel and Notation)

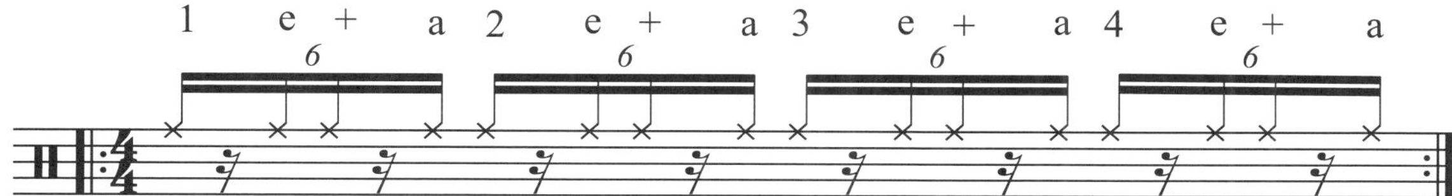

(Although the patterns that are listed are on the hi-hat, this procedure applies to hi-hat, snare and bass Drum too.)

Section 2A
One-Bar Phrases

Pop Rock Loop 1   Feel____________

CD 1 (36)

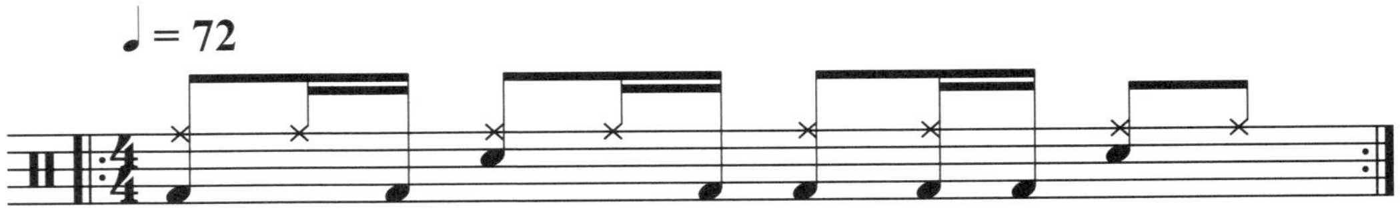

$\quad$ = 72

Pop Rock Loop 2   Feel____________

CD 1 (37)

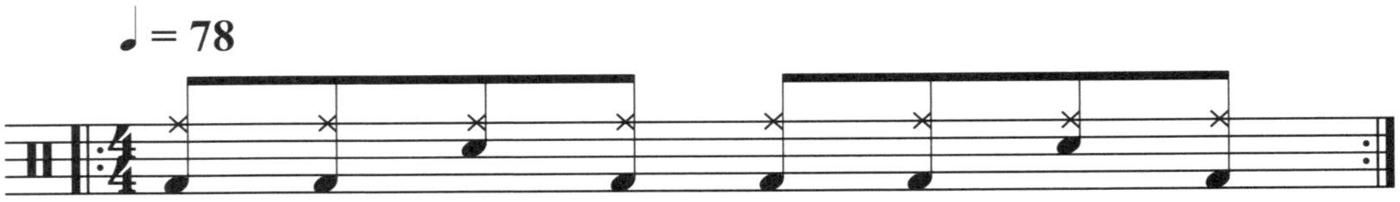

$\quad$ = 78

Two-Bar Phrases

Pop Rock Loop 1a   Feel____________

CD 1 (38)

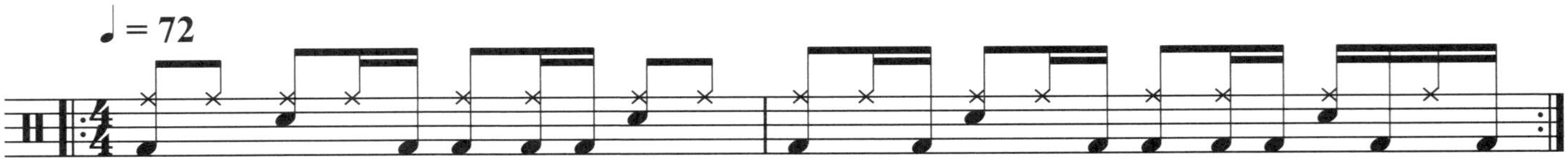

$\quad$ = 72

Pop Rock Loop 2a   Feel____________

CD 1 (39)

$\quad$ = 78

Section 2B
One-Bar Phrases

Pop Rock Loop 3 Feel_____________

CD 1 40

Pop Rock Loop 4 Feel_____________

CD 1 41

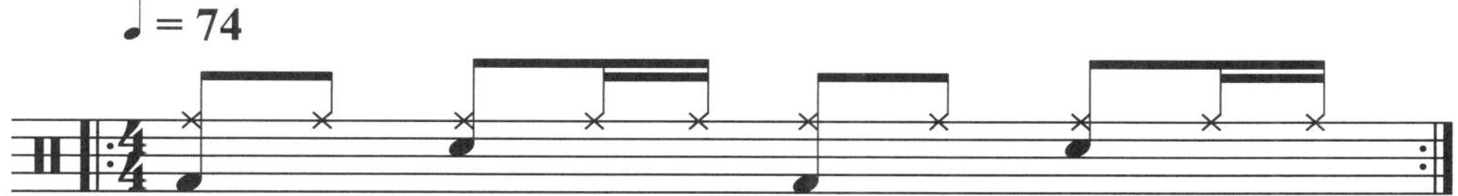

Two-Bar Phrases

Pop Rock Loop 3a Feel_____________

CD 1 42

Pop Rock Loop 4a Feel_____________

CD 1 43

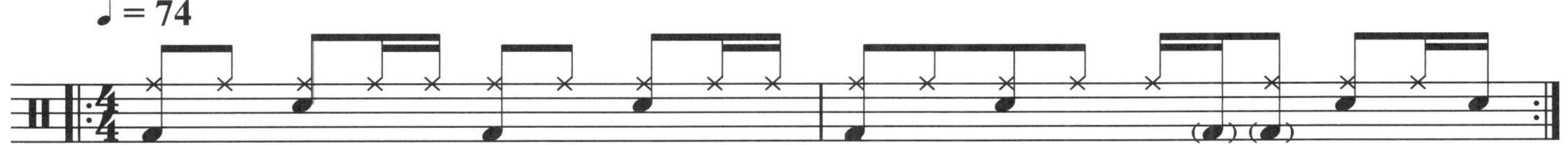

Section 2C
One-Bar Phrases

Pop Rock Loop 5 Feel______________

CD 1 **44**

Pop Rock Loop 6 Feel______________

CD 1 **45**

Two-Bar Phrases

Pop Rock Loop 5a Feel______________

CD 1 **46**

Pop Rock Loop 6a Feel______________

CD 1 **47**

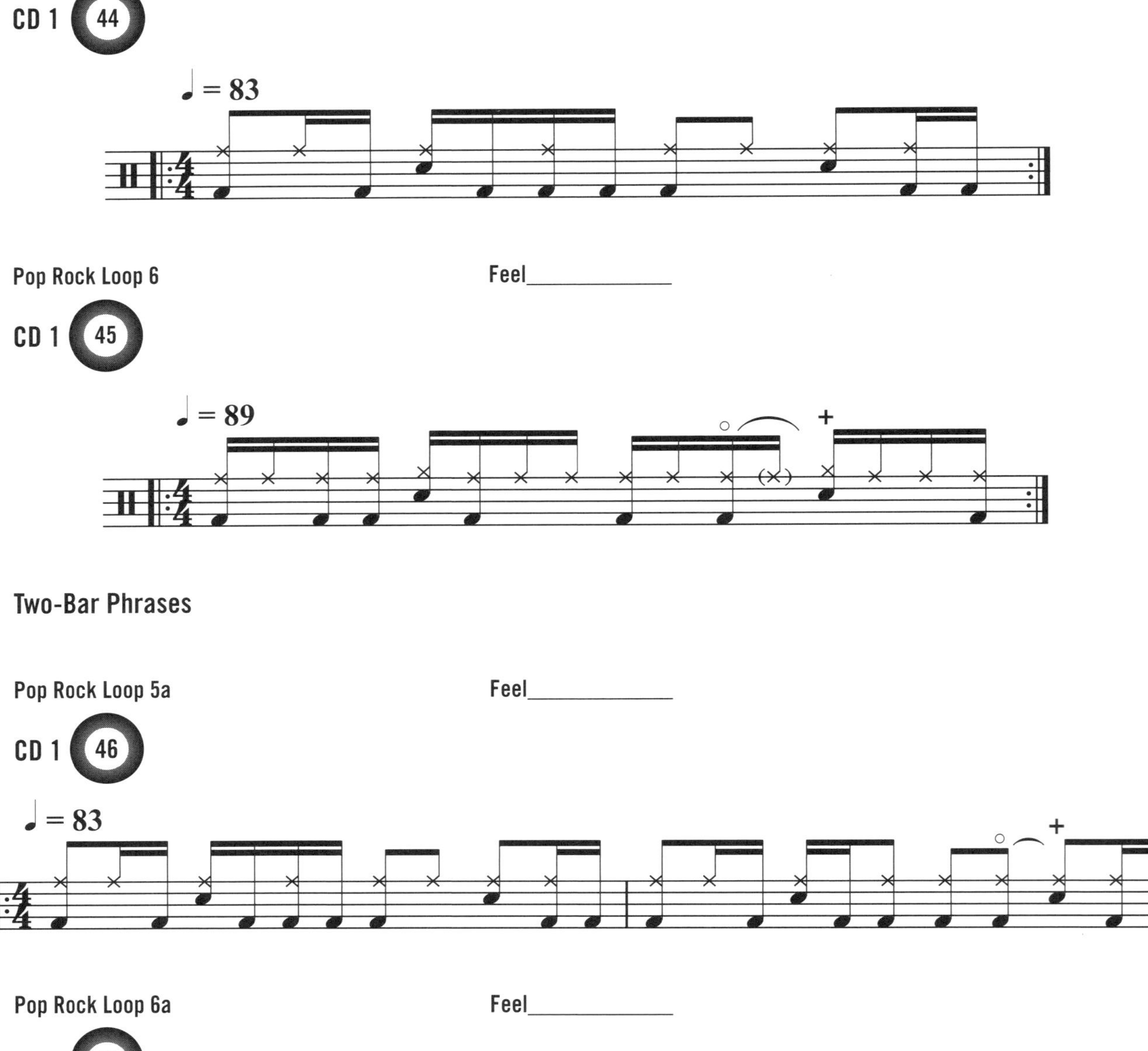

Section 2D
One-Bar Phrases

Pop Rock Loop 7 Feel____________

CD 1 48

Pop Rock Loop 8 Feel____________

CD 1 49

Two-Bar Phrases

Pop Rock Loop 7a Feel____________

CD 1 50

Pop Rock Loop 8a Feel____________

CD 1 51

Section 2E
One-Bar Phrases

Pop Rock Loop 9  Feel_______________

**Total Accompaniment Reminder: There are many bass-drum
notes in this loop:** *"When in doubt, leave it out".*

CD 1 52

Pop Rock Loop 10 Feel_______________

CD 1 53

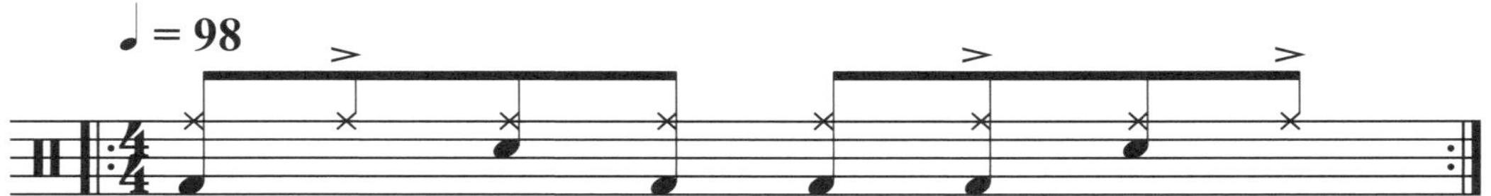

Two-Bar Phrases

Pop Rock Loop 9a  Feel_______________

CD 1 54

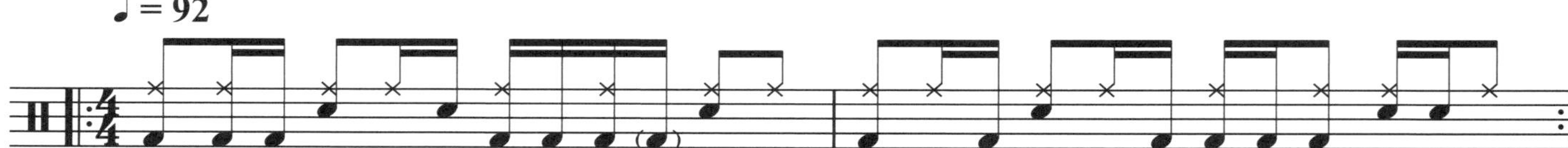

Pop Rock Loop 10a  Feel_______________

CD 1 55

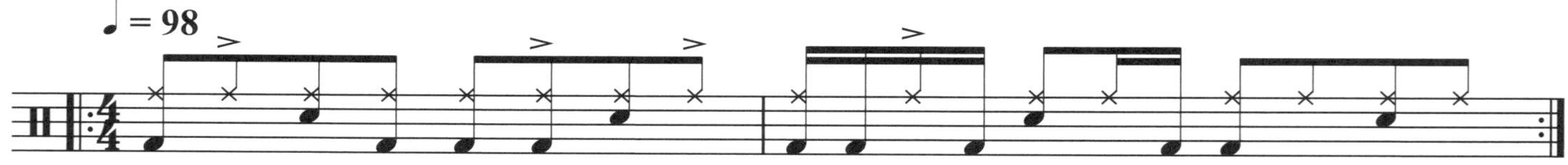

Section 2F
One-Bar Phrases

Pop Rock Loop 11   Feel_____________

CD 1 56

$\quad = 90$

Pop Rock Loop 12   Feel_____________

CD 1 57

$\quad = 96$

Two-Bar Phrases

Pop Rock Loop 11a   Feel_____________

CD 1 58

$\quad = 90$

Pop Rock Loop 12a   Feel_____________

Notation Reminder: Notice the crash cymbal on beat 4 of measure 2.

CD 1 59

$\quad = 96$

Section 2G
One-Bar Phrases

Pop Rock Loop 13 Feel______________

CD 1   60

$\quarternote = 100$

Pop Rock Loop 14 Feel______________

CD 1   61

$\quarternote = 109$

Two-Bar Phrases

Pop Rock Loop 13a Feel______________

CD 1   62

$\quarternote = 100$

Pop Rock Loop 14a Feel______________

CD 1   63

$\quarternote = 109$

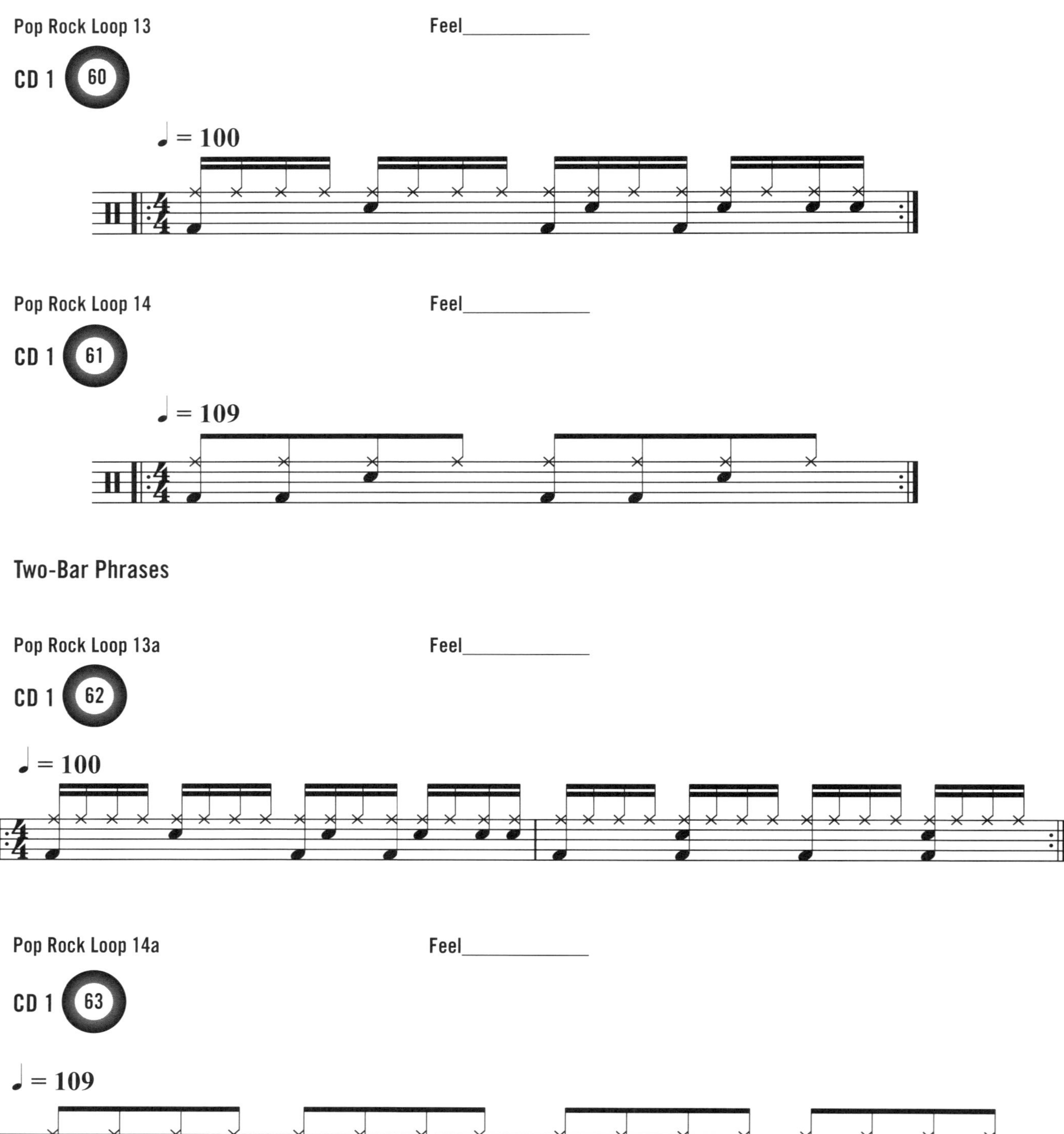

Section 2H
One-Bar Phrases

Pop Rock Loop 15　　　　　　　　　Feel_______________

CD 1 64

♩ = 103

Pop Rock Loop 16　　　　　　　　Feel_______________Beat Placement_______________

CD 1 65

♩ = 107

Two-Bar Phrases

Pop Rock Loop 15a　　　　　　　　Feel_______________

CD 1 66

♩ = 103

Pop Rock Loop 16a　　　　　　　　Feel_______________

CD 1 67

♩ = 107

Pop Rock
One Bar Combination Solo

CD 1  68

Pop Rock
Two Bar Combination Solo

CD 1  69

♩ = 100

(Continued on next page)

(Continued)

Feel Answers

Feel Key
ST= Straight Feel
SW= Swing Feel

One-Bar Phrases	**Two-Bar Phrases**
Pop Rock Loop 1 = ST	Pop Rock Loop 1a = ST
Pop Rock Loop 2 = ST	Pop Rock Loop 2a = ST
Pop Rock Loop 3 = ST	Pop Rock Loop 3a = ST
Pop Rock Loop 4 = ST	Pop Rock Loop 4a = ST
Pop Rock Loop 5 = SW	Pop Rock Loop 5a = SW
Pop Rock Loop 6 = SW	Pop Rock Loop 6a = SW
Pop Rock Loop 7 = SW	Pop Rock Loop 7a = SW
Pop Rock Loop 8 = SW	Pop Rock Loop 8a = SW
Pop Rock Loop 9 = ST	Pop Rock Loop 9a = ST
Pop Rock Loop 10 = ST	Pop Rock Loop 10a = ST
Pop Rock Loop 11= ST	Pop Rock Loop 11a = ST
Pop Rock Loop 12 = ST	Pop Rock Loop 12a = ST
Pop Rock Loop 13= SW	Pop Rock Loop 13a = SW
Pop Rock Loop 14 = SW	Pop Rock Loop 14a = SW
Pop Rock Loop 15 = SW	Pop Rock Loop 15a = SW
Pop Rock Loop 16 = SW	Pop Rock Loop 16a = SW

Total Accompaniment:
An Additional Practice Method for Chapters 1 and 2.

The Radio Treatment

Now we understand what Metal, Rock and Pop loops sound like, the roles they play in music, and how to approach playing with them. We also need to know how these loops function in the real world of live performance and/or recording. Therefore, how can we sound authentic and musical while performing with them? Just like learning any other musical genre, the best way to grasp these concepts is to study the current recordings that utilize these elements. In addition, all of the Metal, Rock and Pop recordings that do use loops usually follow the same common arrangement style. I call this arrangement style *The Radio Treatment*.

This arrangement style is used quite frequently in today's Metal, Rock and Pop recordings. More often than not, the first eight-bar section (the Verse) is a loop playing alone and extremely quiet. Subsequently, as if out of nowhere, the acoustic drums enter (without a transition fill) into the second eight-bar section (the Chorus). This technique, along with the absence of an introduction fill, presents a huge contrast of texture between the Verse and Chorus of a song. In addition, this treatment adds energy and excitement to a song's most important section: the Chorus.

Now that we understand this new arrangement style, please go back through Chapters 1 and 2 and play them in the following format:

Radio Practice Example

Take any loop from Chapters 1 and 2 (Rock and Metal or Pop Rock loops) and use the following practice format: eight bars of Verse (rest) and eight bars of grooving in the Chorus. Thus, you will be practicing a sixteen-bar phrase.

Radio Example with Pop Rock Loop 9: CD1 Track 70 Demonstration. (CD1 Track 52 Play along)

Remember not to play a Transition Fill into the Chorus!

CD 1 70 (CD1 2 PLAY ALONG)

Acoustic Drums Play with the Loop in the Chorus

Chapter 3: Hip Hop and R&B Loops
65–95 bpm
Straight Eighth- and Sixteenth-Note Feels, Swing Feels and Broken Time Feels

Hip Hop is a musical genre that deconstructs familiar sounds and songs and recreates them as entirely new and unpredictable songs. Early Hip Hop records (Old School R&B) were made by DJs scratching records with MCs rapping over the resulting rhythms. As the style progressed, the scratching techniques were replaced by digital sampling, beat making and looping. With their dense collages of samples, beats, loops and scratching, Hip Hop became and is now one of the dominant forms of music heard on the radio.

There are three sections in this chapter:
- **Section 3A** focuses on both straight and swing loops at 85 bpm. In addition, the grooves are based on eighth-note hi-hat patterns with the snare on beats 2 and 4.
- **Section 3B** focuses on straight eighth-and sixteenth-note grooves at tempos 65–94 bpm. In addition, the loops have both eighth and sixteenth hi-hat grooves with the snare on beats 2 and 4.
- **Section 3C** focuses on straight eighth- and sixteenth-note grooves at tempos 67–90 bpm. Furthermore, they contain broken-time feels (broken-time feels feature snare patterns that do not always fall on beats 2 and 4, and the hi-hat is usually not playing a constant eighth or sixteenth pattern either).

All three sections utilize one-bar phrases.

In Section 3A:
Just as in the previous chapter, follow the feel, counting, clapping and analysis methods from Fundamentals 2A and 2B (Feel and Beat Placement). Then write in either straight or swing feel and ahead, in the middle or behind the beat in the space provided. For example:

Feel______________Beat Placement______________
(Answers are provided on page 53)

In Sections 3B and 3C:
Just as in the previous chapter, follow the counting, clapping and analysis methods from Fundamental 2B (Beat Placement). Then write in ahead, in the middle or behind the beat in the space provided. For example:

Beat Placement______________
(Answers are provided on page 53)

Total Accompaniment Duration and Note Choice Hint:
The Hip Hop Backbeat

Most Hip Hop tracks heard on the radio are programmed at a medium tempo and feature an extremely wide backbeat. This *wide* backbeat consists of many layered claps and snare sounds; this not only makes the groove feel huge, but it also makes it *very* difficult to find the center of beats 2 and 4. Thus, it may be difficult to line up with many of the Hip Hop loop examples that utilize these textures.

So how can you fix this and line up with each Hip Hop loop example?

Well, let's take a listen to **Hip Hop Loop 2: CD1 Track** **71** **Demonstration.** (CD1 Track **73** Play along)

CD 1 **71**

As you listen to this loop, you will undoubtedly notice that there is a wide backbeat that employs many claps and snare sounds on 2 and 4. These sounds give the impression that there is a room full of people clapping their hands to the groove.

How can you possibly imitate a room full of people clapping their hands?

Well, what usually happens when two (or more) people try to clap together in unison? Do they line up exactly? Of course not; they are usually "a bit off" from one another! Therefore, this causes the beats to flam with one another. **So there is your answer: play a flam on beats 2 and 4 to imitate a clapping sound!**

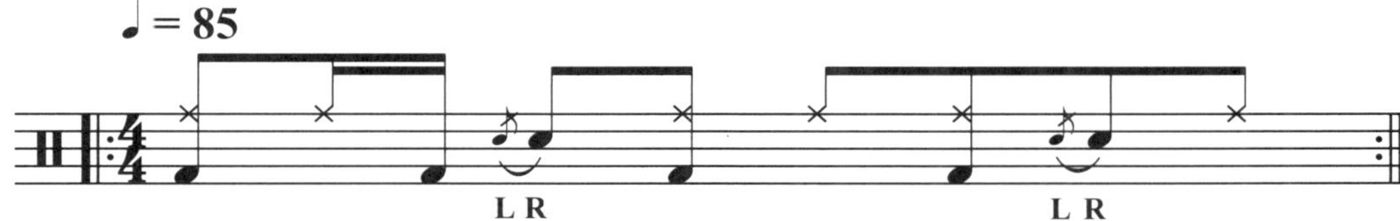

Therefore, anytime you hear a loop that has an extremely wide (clap-like) backbeat, try playing snare flams on beats 2 and 4.

Section 3A: 85 bpm

Hip Hop Loop 1   Feel_____________Beat Placement_____________

CD 1 (72)

Hip Hop Loop 2   Feel_____________Beat Placement_____________

CD 1 (73)

Hip Hop Loop 3   Feel_____________Beat Placement_____________

CD 1 (74)

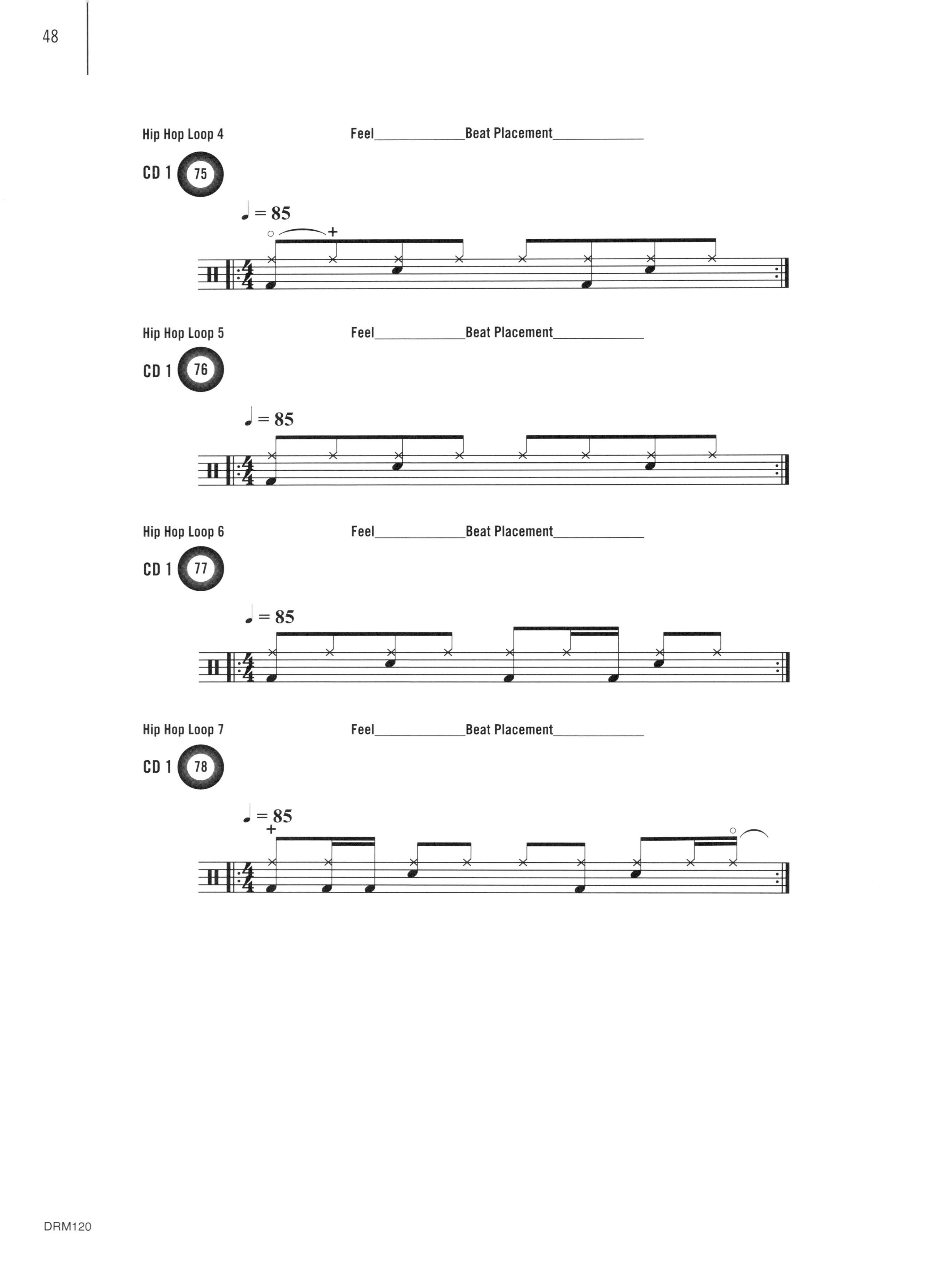

Hip Hop Loop 4

Feel_______________ Beat Placement_______________

CD 1 **75**

♩ = 85

Hip Hop Loop 5

Feel_______________ Beat Placement_______________

CD 1 **76**

♩ = 85

Hip Hop Loop 6

Feel_______________ Beat Placement_______________

CD 1 **77**

♩ = 85

Hip Hop Loop 7

Feel_______________ Beat Placement_______________

CD 1 **78**

♩ = 85

Hip Hop Loop 8

Feel_____________Beat Placement_____________

CD 2 (1)

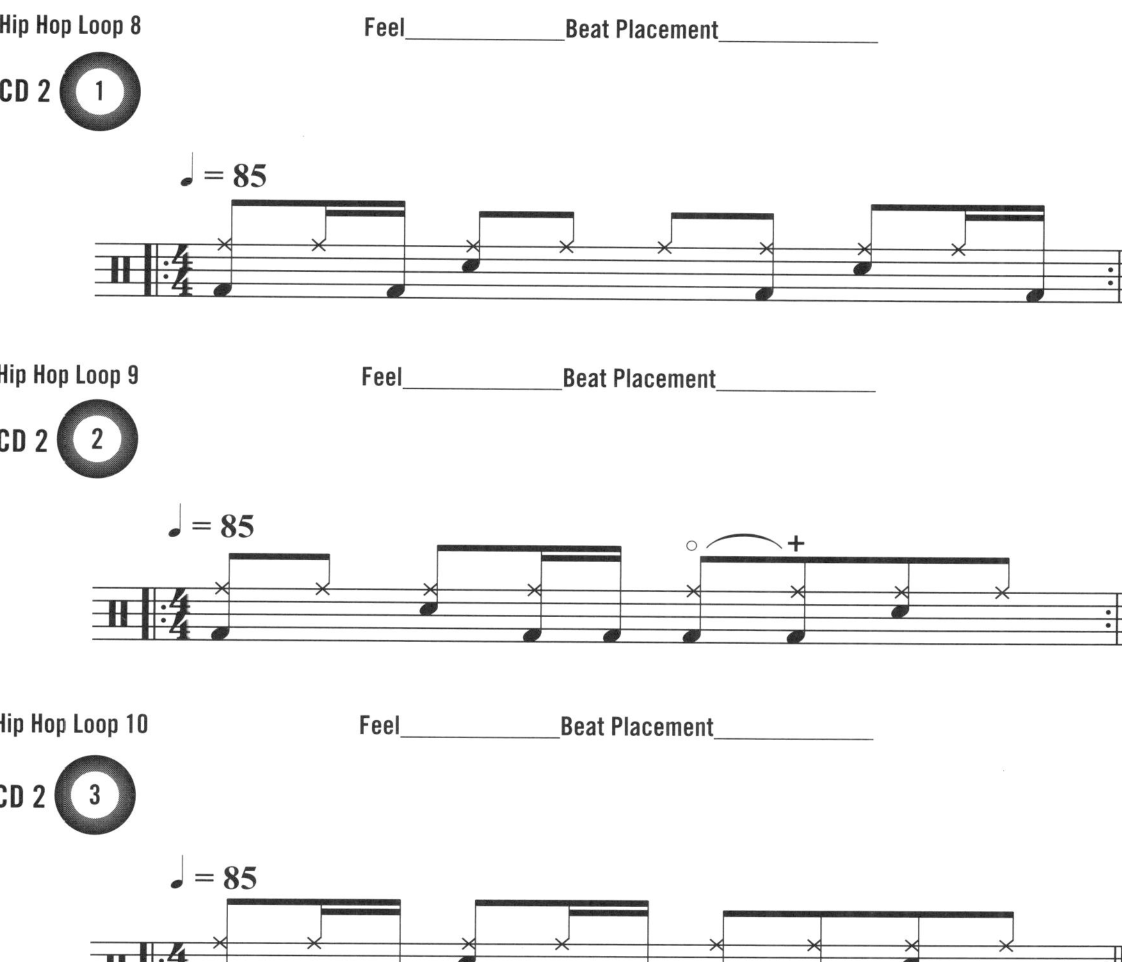

Section 3B: Straight Feel (65–94 bpm, Eighth and Sixteenth Hi-hat)

Hip Hop Loop 11   **Beat Placement**_____________

CD 2 (4)

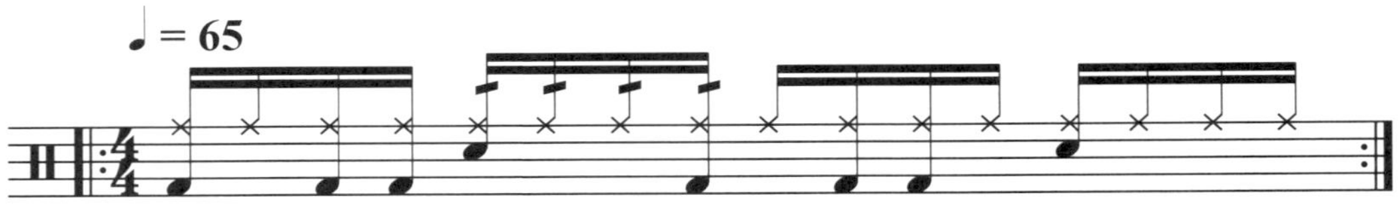

$\quad$ = 65

Hip Hop Loop 12   **Beat Placement**_____________

Notation Reminder – Double Stroke

In the case of this loop, it actually turns the "+ and a"of beat 2 into thirty-second notes.

CD 2 (5)

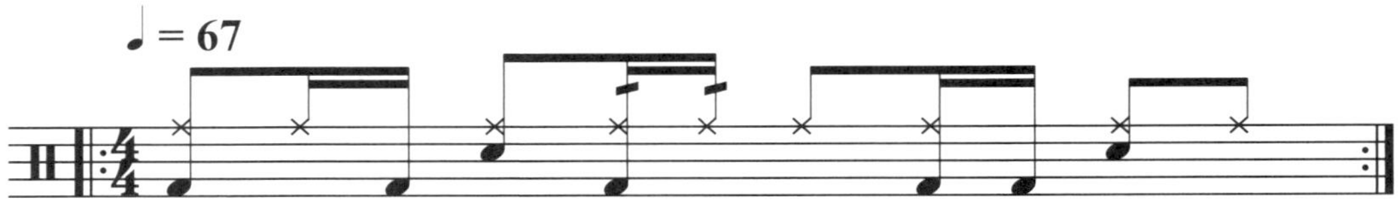

$\quad$ = 67

Hip Hop Loop 13   **Beat Placement**_____________

CD 2 (6)

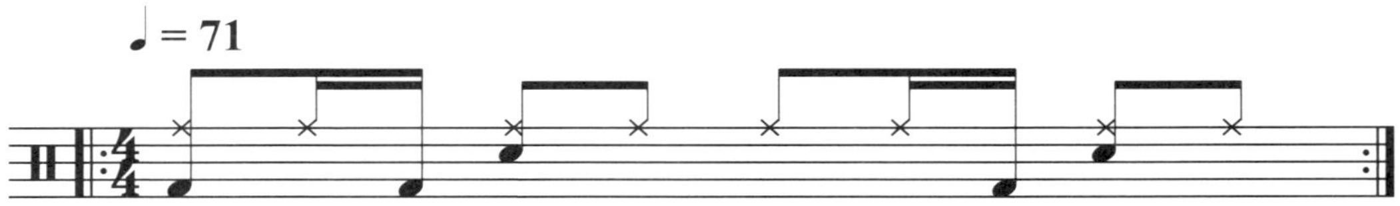

$\quad$ = 71

Hip Hop Loop 14   **Beat Placement**_____________

CD 2 (7)

$\quad$ = 75

Notice the keyboards hits written in the hi-hat part as accents.

Hip Hop Loop 15 Beat Placement________________

CD 2 (8)

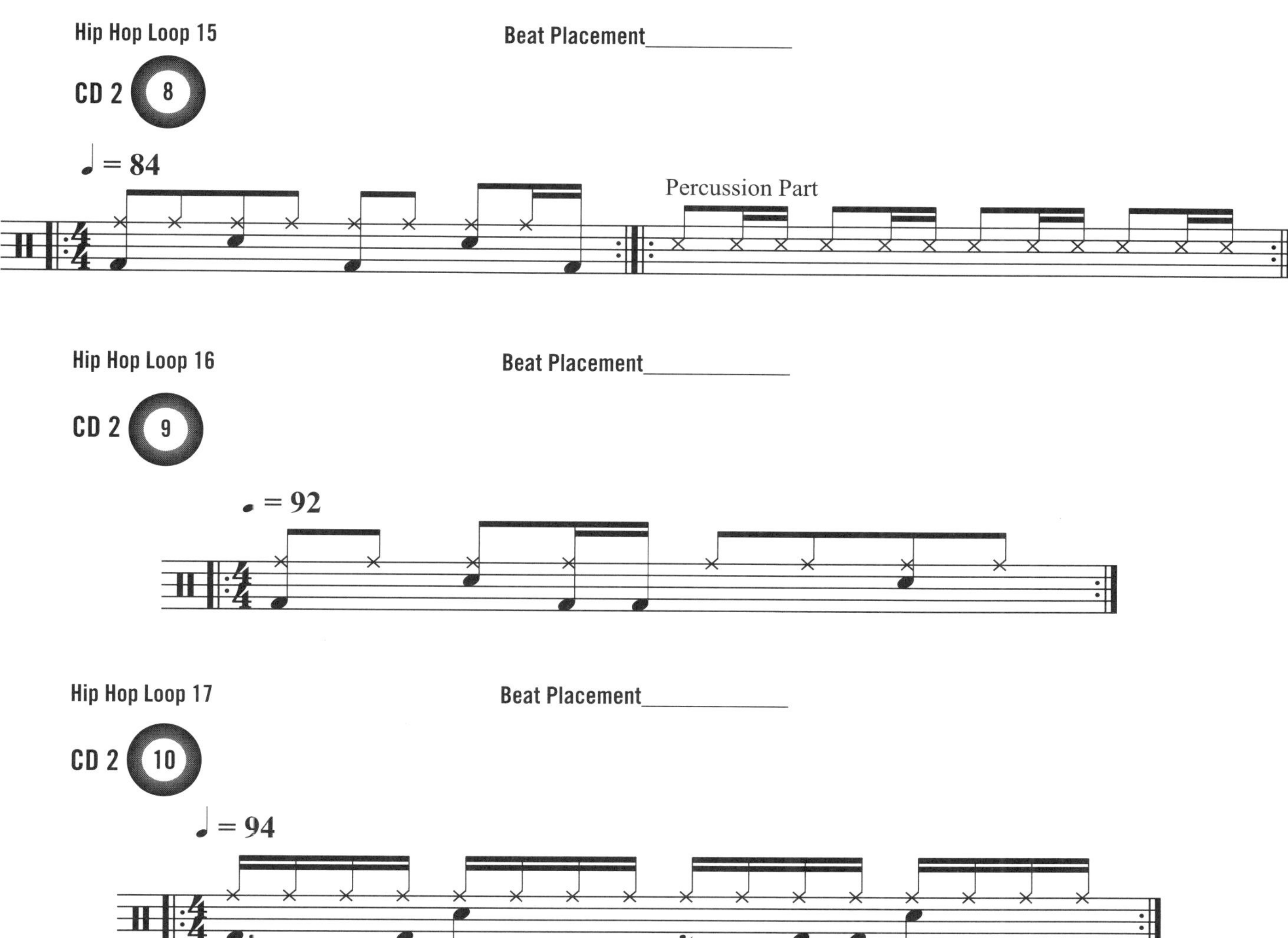

Hip Hop Loop 16 Beat Placement________________

CD 2 (9)

Hip Hop Loop 17 Beat Placement________________

CD 2 (10)

Section 3C: Straight Feel (67–90 bpm, Broken Feels)

When you are playing (or listening) to Hip Hop's broken-feel grooves, you'll notice that the hi-hat and snare patterns are not common, static (i.e., repeating) phrases, as in the Rock and Metal or Pop Rock chapters.

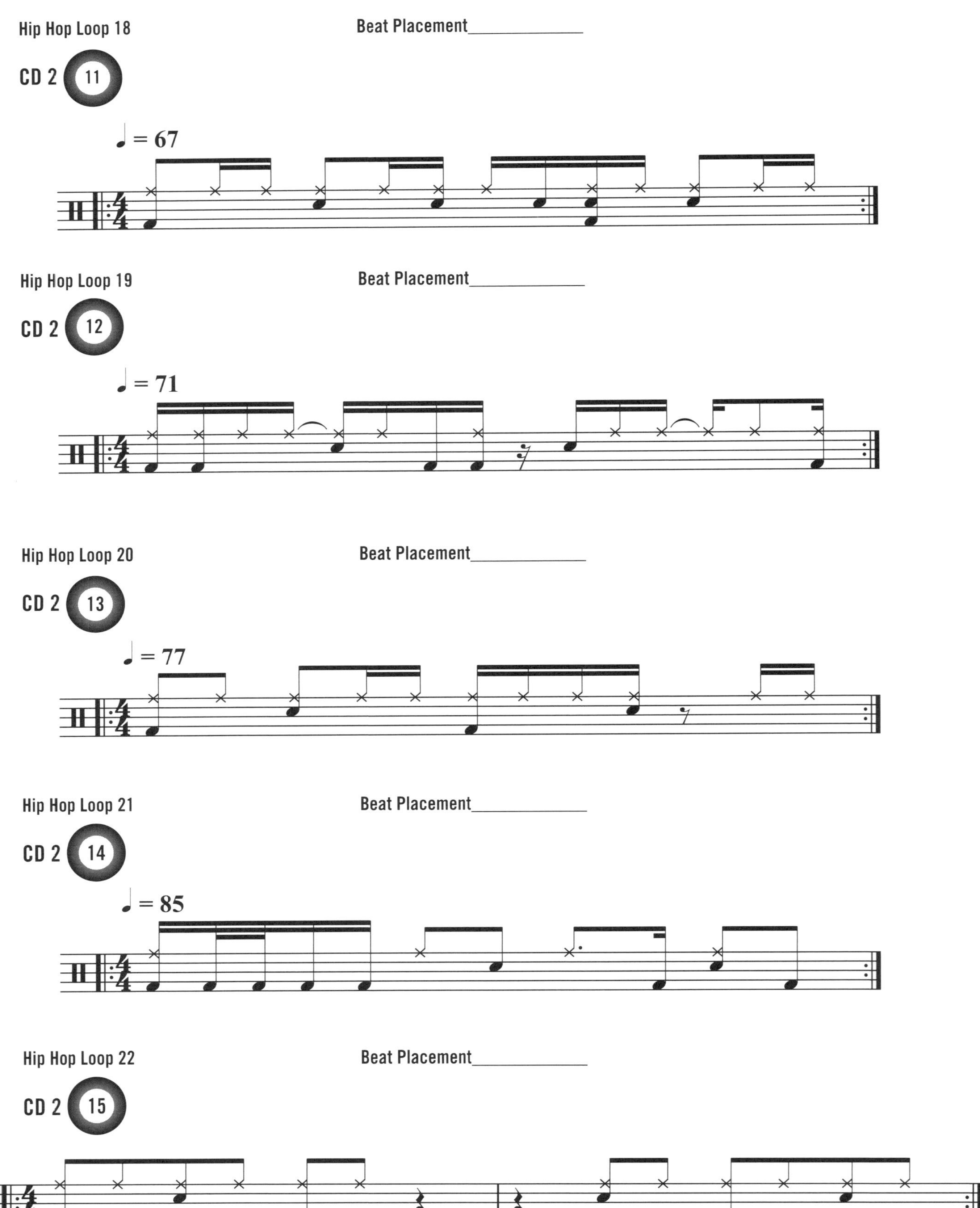

Hip Hop Loops, Beat Placement and Feel Answers

Beat Placement Key
AH = Ahead of the Beat
Mid = Middle of the Beat
BH= Behind the Beat

Feel Key
ST= Straight Feel
SW = Swing Feel

Section 1 (3A)	Section 2 (3B)	Section 3 (3C)
Hip Hop Loop 1 = ST, MID	Hip Hop Loop 11 = BH	Hip Hop Loop 18 = BH
Hip Hop Loop 2 = ST, AH	Hip Hop Loop 12 = BH	Hip Hop Loop 19 = MID
Hip Hop Loop 3 = ST, MID	Hip Hop Loop 13 = BH	Hip Hop Loop 20 = BH
Hip Hop Loop 4 = ST, BH	Hip Hop Loop 14 = AH	Hip Hop Loop 21 = MID
Hip Hop Loop 5 = ST, BH	Hip Hop Loop 15 = BH	Hip Hop Loop 22 - MID
Hip Hop Loop 6 = SW, BH	Hip Hop Loop 16 = MID	
Hip Hop Loop 7 = SW, BH	Hip Hop Loop 17 = AH	
Hip Hop Loop 8 = SW, BH		
Hip Hop Loop 9 = SW, BH		
Hip Hop Loop 10 = SW, BH		

Stylistic considerations in Hip Hop: Most Hip Hop grooves are __________ and in the __________ of the beat. Furthermore, they also feature both ____________ and _____________ feels.

Answers: Behind, Middle, Straight and Swing

Total Accompaniment:
An Additional Practice Method for All Loop Types

Drop Outs

Drop Outs were created in the DJ (and producer) culture, and they are created by pressing the mute button on a mixing console while the drum groove is playing. This silences the entire drum groove and serves to accentuate and highlight a particular element (such as a vocal line or sound effect) in a composition.

From a drummer's standpoint, these drop outs occur on an odd place in the beat (from what drummers are commonly used to). For example, instead of dropping out (or resting) from beat 1 to beat 1 of a two- measure phrase, this technique allows you to drop out on any given beat (and measure) and return into the groove at any given point (in the beat) as well.

A Note on the Drop-Out Exercises

The drop-out exercises will help you develop the proper vocabulary and *thought process*, and ultimately help you to perform drop outs like a DJ. In order to understand this method, work through these exercises with any loop from the previous three chapters.

Before you get started, here are three essential thoughts:

- **Thought 1**
  "Drop out" of the groove prior to the downbeat. When you perform the rest (drop out), it is extremely important that you "pull out" of the groove prior to the downbeat to give the illusion of being muted.

- **Thought 2**
  Restart within the Groove. When you resume the groove, you must actually start at the exact return point within the groove, as if you are a loop being "muted" on a mixer. For example, if you were to drop out on the "+" of beat 3 and must return on beat 2 of the next measure, it would be played like this.

CD 2 **16**

If you still do not understand what it sounds like to be muted, play a CD on your stereo system. As the music is playing, quickly turn down the volume knob for approximately one second. Then, quickly turn it up again. Do you hear how the music is playing as if it had never been turned down? It is playing exactly where it had left off, just like being muted.

- **Thought 3**
  No Return Accents. As drummers we have been brainwashed to always play a cymbal crash heading into a section (or beat 1) of a song. However, in these exercises you must resist that temptation. **Do not play an accent (or cymbal crash) when you return into the groove.** This gives the illusion that you are a sampled and/or looped groove that is being muted.

Drop-Out Key

| Play time or time fragment | Drop out where the quarter rest falls | Continue grooving |

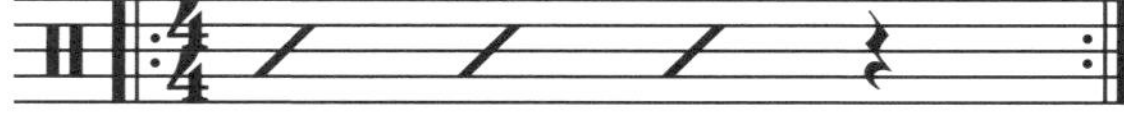

One Measure Drop Outs

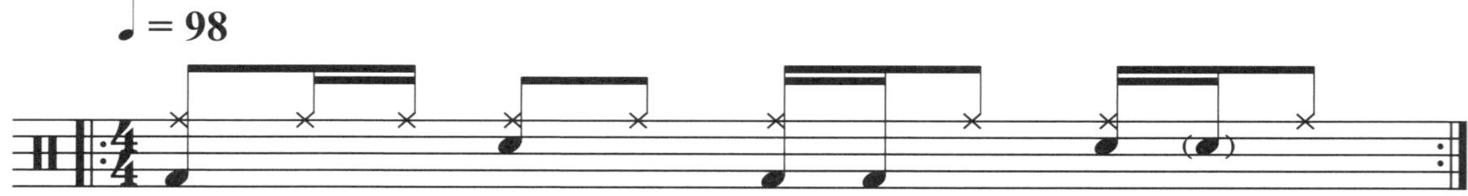

Here is a demonstration of how to work through the one-measure drop-out exercises:

1. First, pick a one-measure drop-out exercise. In this case, let's choose Drop-Out Exercise No. 1.

2. Secondly, pick a loop to perform with. This time, let's choose the one-bar example from Rock and Metal Loop 3.

♩ = 98

3. Lastly, now play the groove during the time slashes and drop out for the quarter-note rest. (Remember that the loop will be playing during the rest). The exercise is played like this: **CD2 Track 17 Demonstration.**

CD 2 17

Rock & Metal Loop 3, phrased within Drop out Example 1

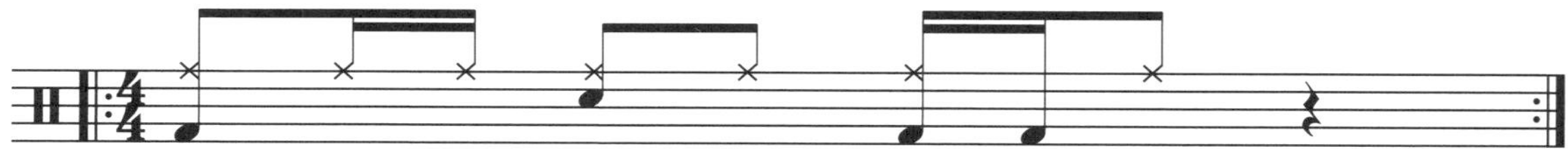

Once you have mastered any one of the Drop-Out Exercises, pick any loop in the previous chapters and practice any Drop-Out Exercise (Nos. 1–15) with one of the following Drop-Out Practice Methods.

Drop-Out Practice Methods

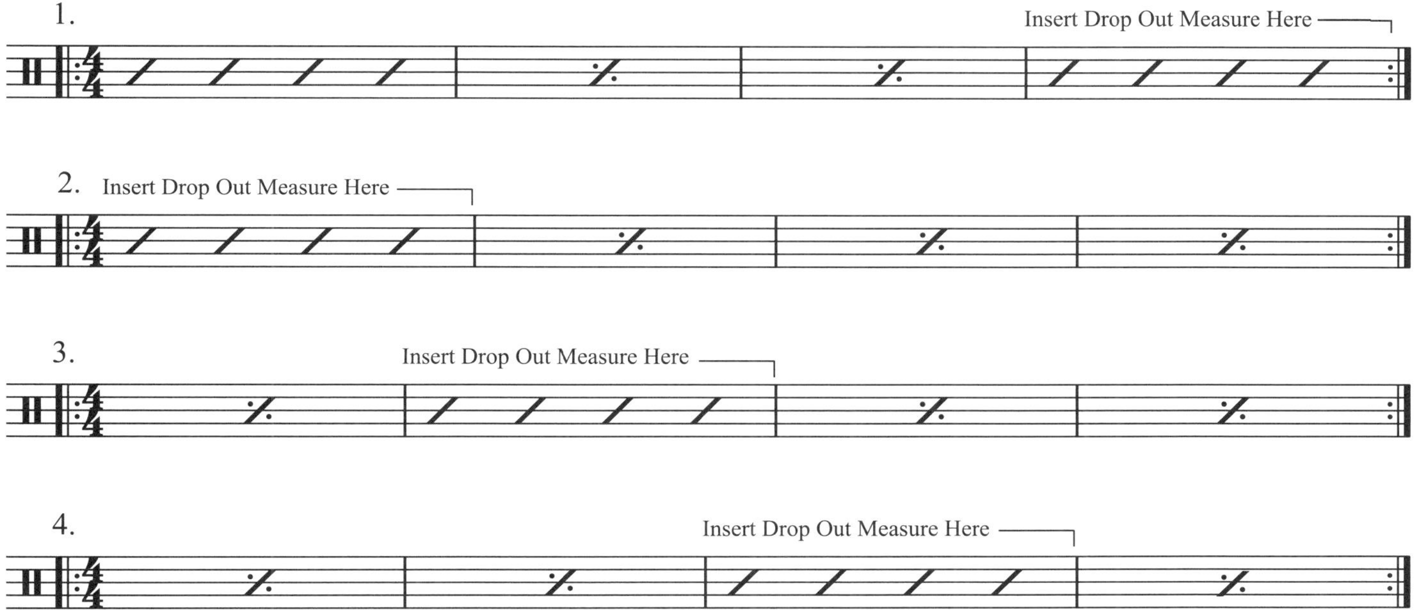

Here is a demonstration of how to work through the previously mentioned Drop-Out Practice Methods (along with one of the Drop-Out Exercises).

1. First, pick a Drop-Out Exercise. In this case, let's choose Drop-Out Exercise No. 1 once more.

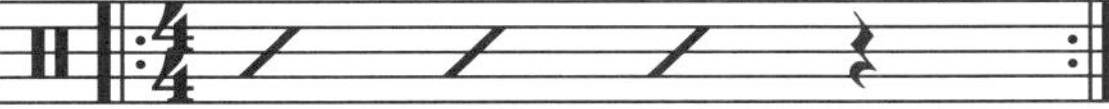

2. Second, choose a loop example to perform with as well. For the sake of familiarity, let's choose the one-bar example of Rock and Metal Loop 3.

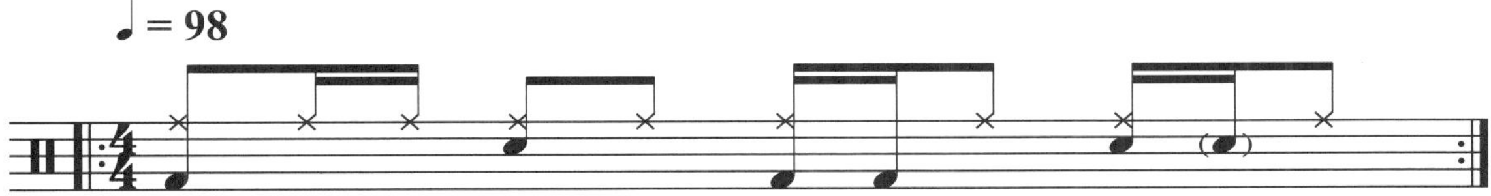

3. Third, pick one of the four Drop-Out Practice Methods too. In this case let's choose number one:

4. Lastly, play three bars of time along with a Loop and on the fourth Bar execute the Drop Out Exercise. (Remember that the Loop will be playing during the Rest). The Exercise is played like this.

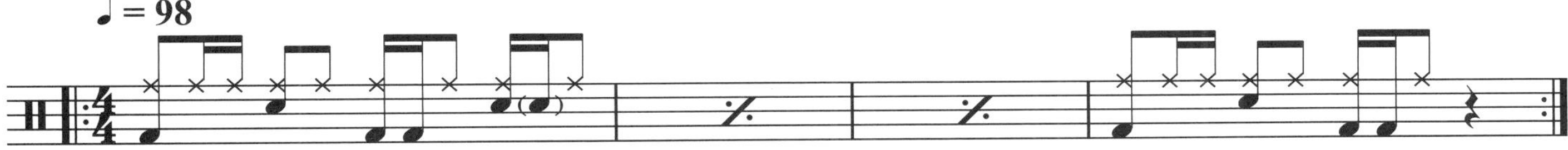

Repeat this process for whichever Drop-Out Exercise and Drop-Out Practice Method you choose.

Total Accompaniment:
An Additional Practice Method for ALL LOOP Types

Fills

When you attempt to play fills, keep in mind that the audience does not realize (or care) that you are performing with loops. Therefore, you should strive to blend your parts (and fills) with the loop and its melody.

How can you blend with the loop and keep the momentum going, in addition to playing a great transition fill?

- **Thought 1**
  Well, what item is present in nearly all of the previous loop examples (except for the Hip Hop broken feels)? Answer: **the backbeat!** So every time you fill, it should include the backbeat in some shape or form. This important fill trait will help you blend seamlessly with the loop. Furthermore, any additional notes that you play should be within the melody and groove of the loop. **(sixteenth-note groove = eighth- or sixteenth-based fill = Fundamental 3 "Momentum" = fill choices)**

- **Thought 2**
  Keep your fills short in duration. A fill that is more than one measure can definitely detract from the overall groove structure. Therefore, it would be more advantageous to play fills that are one, two, three or four beats in length.

- **Thought 3**
  Note choice is important too. Fills that are on the hi-hat/cymbals are also less likely to detract from the loop. In order to completely blend with the loop, stay away from the snare during fills, unless it is to play the backbeat.

Notation Addition (for the Fills section)
Fill Key

The Fill Exercises on the following page will help you develop the proper independence, vocabulary and *ultimately* help you to include the backbeat in your fills. Feel free to experiment with many different stickings as well.

Backbeat Based-Snare and Tom Based Fill Exercises
Two-beat fragments

Work through these exercises with a comfortable loop, your bass drum playing quarter notes and your hi-hat foot closing on beats 2 and 4 with the backbeat.

Here is an example with Fill Exercise No. 4.

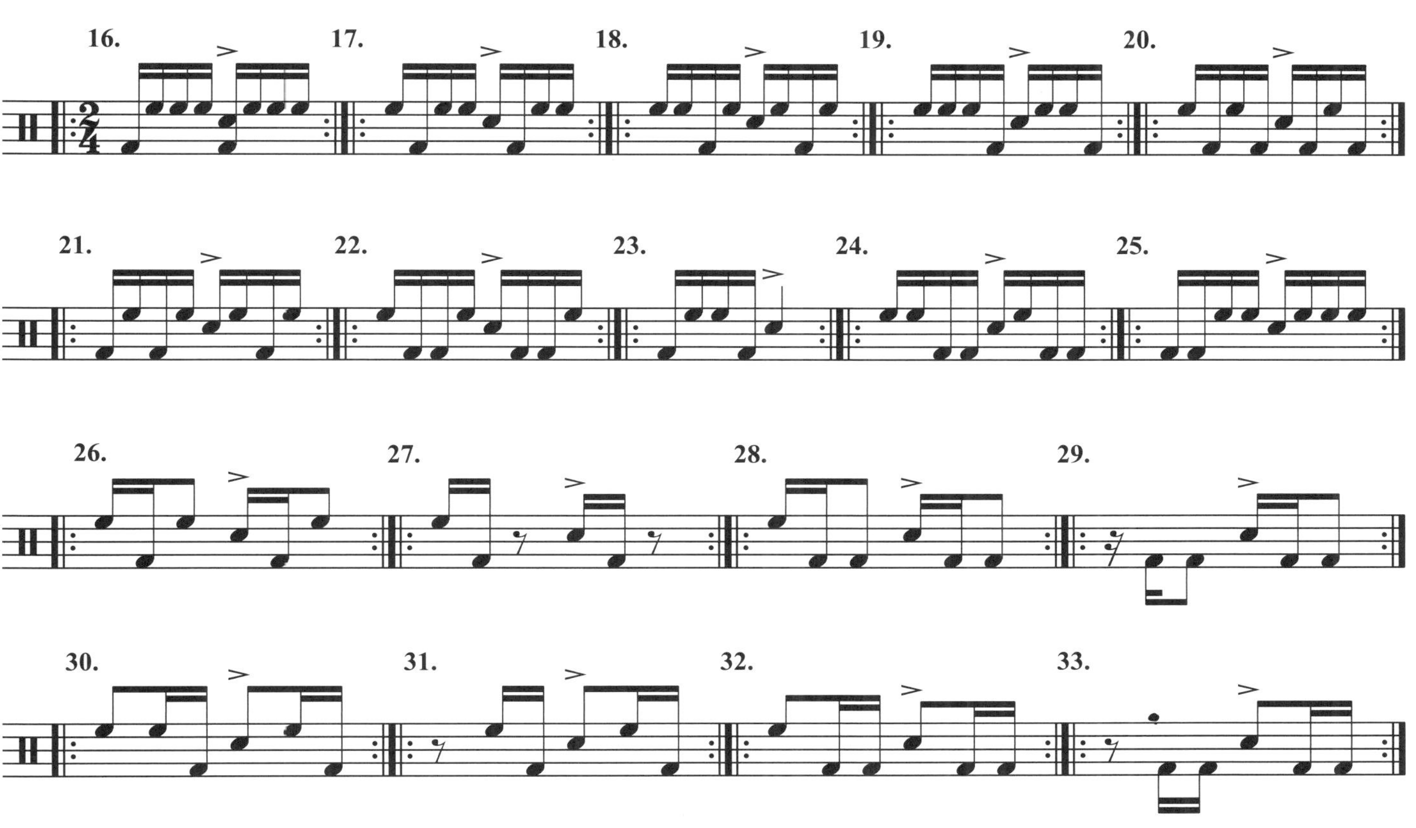

Backbeat-Based Hand and Foot Combination Fill Exercises: 2 Beat Fragments

Work through these exercises with a comfortable loop, with your hi-hat foot closing on beats 2 and 4 with the backbeat or on all four quarter notes.

Fills Practice Method

Once you have mastered any one of the fill exercises, pick any loop in the previous chapters and practice your fills with one of the following three Fill Practice Methods. In the first example, you will play three bars of time with the loop and then a one-beat fill in measure 4. For example:

Fill Method 1

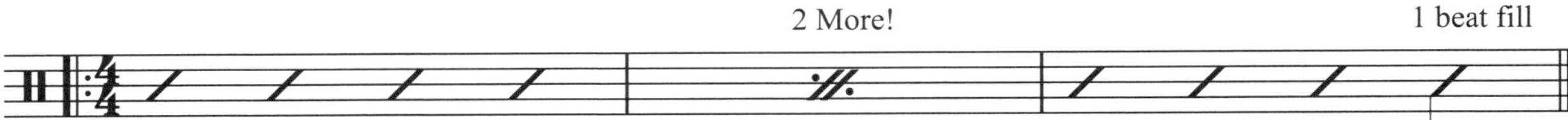

Thus, if you picked Fill Exercise 4 and placed it into Fill Practice Method 1 it would be played as follows:

In examples two, three and four, you will follow the same procedure; these will be fills of either a two-, three- or four-beat length.

Fill Method 2

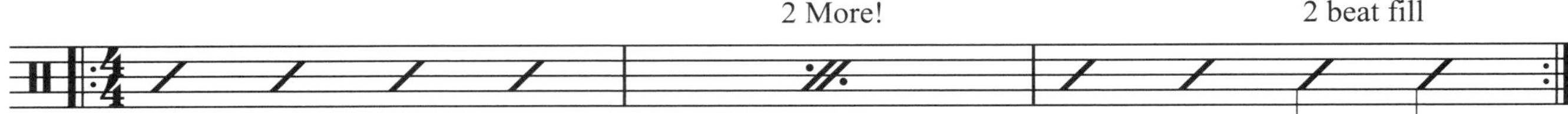

Again, if you picked Fill Exercise 4 and placed it into Fill Practice Method 2 it would be played as follows:

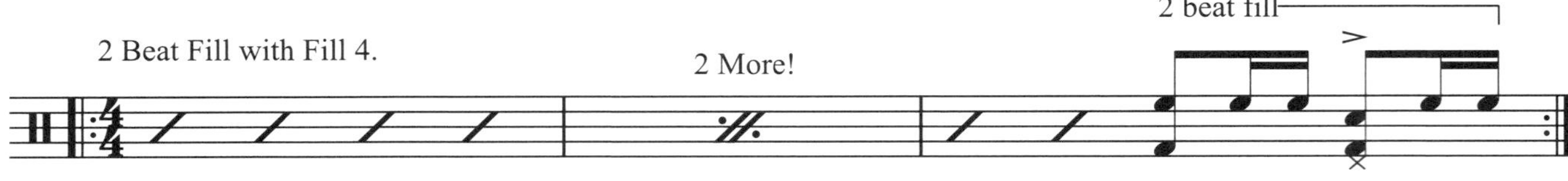

Fill Method 3

Again, if you picked Fill Exercise 4 and placed it into Fill Practice Method 3 it would be played as follows:

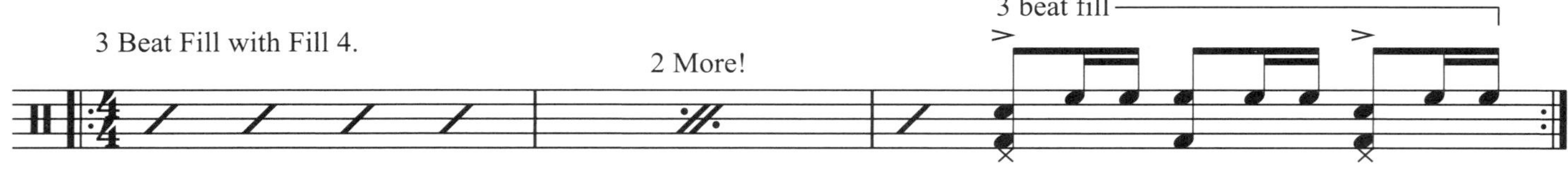

Fill Method 4

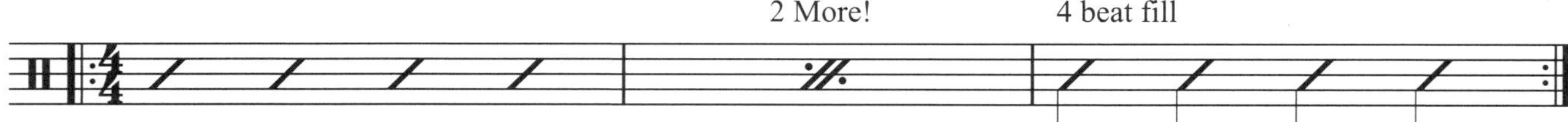

To conclude, if you picked Fill Exercise 4 and placed it into Fill Practice Method 3 it would be played as follows:

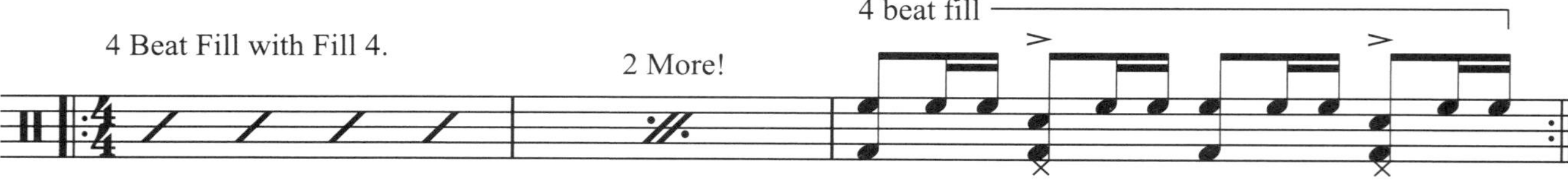

For Example:
Here is an example of all four fill methods (played consecutively) along with

Pop Rock Loop 7

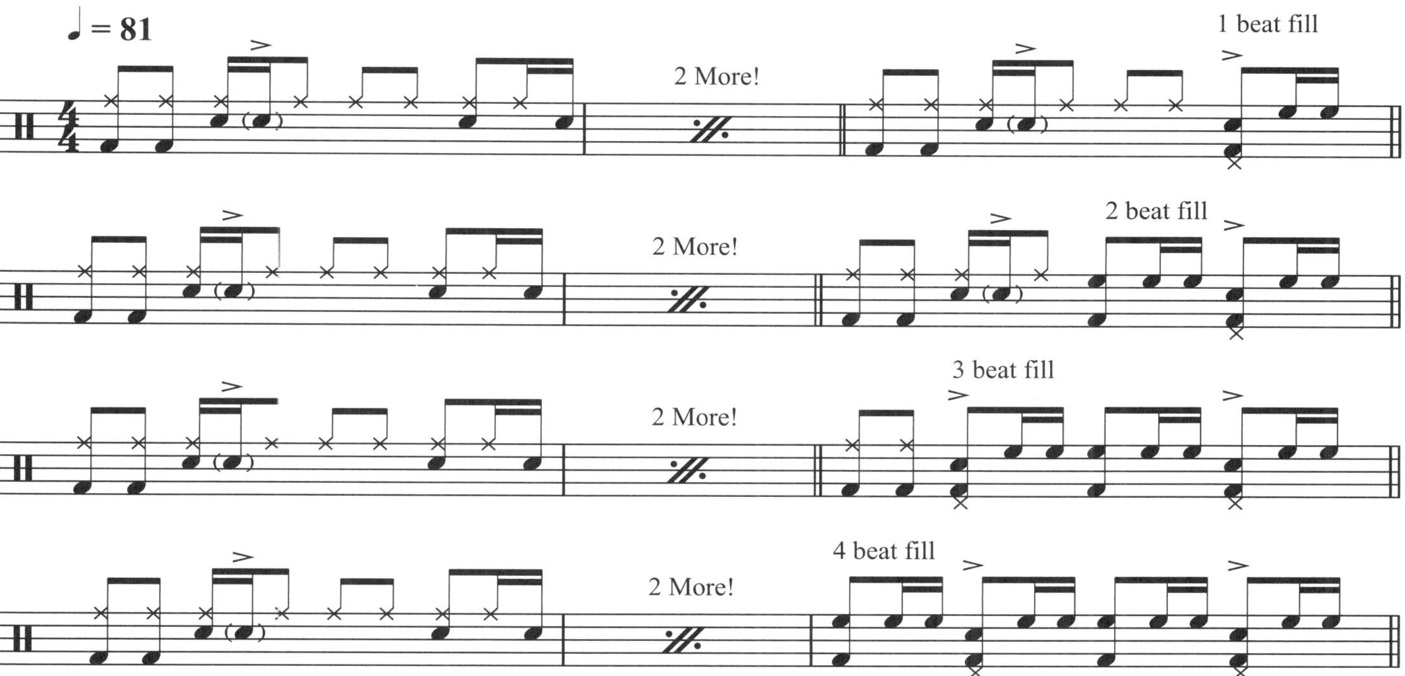

Section 2:
Additional Loop Types

Chapter 4: Percussion Loops
87–110 bpm

Often times, a percussion loop is used not only for rhythmic texture during a recording (or live gig), but as a substitution for a monotonous click track as well. These types of loops help to generate a particular feel and flavor, rather than a specific drum part as in Total Accompaniment. This way the producer (or artist) is not specifically telling you what to play, but they are definitely guiding you in the right direction! In this situation, your job is to keep good time along with a conga part (or shaker, tambourine etc.) and **let the ethnic rhythm influence (and dictate) your drumset groove.**

In this chapter, you will find many different percussion loops. There are conga patterns, shakers, bells, and Tambourines for you to play along with. Sections 4A (Straight Feel) and 4B (Swing Feel) focus on loops between 87–100 bpm.

The Fundamentals 5–8

In addition to the Fundamental Four guidelines presented in Total Accompaniment, here are some additional thoughts to consider when you develop a drumset part alongside a percussion loop.

Fundamental No. 5: Your Groove should follow the percussion loop's accent structure. The accent structure is the groove.

Just as drum loops have a specific bass-drum and snare-drum pattern that we must follow, percussion loops have an accent structure that we must adhere to as well. Therefore, if we neglect to follow this structure, we will not line up or blend well with a percussion loop.

Here is an example. Listen to the **Percussion Loop 1** and try to determine where the loop's accents fall within the beat. Are they on the downbeat, upbeat, or a specific rhythmic figure?

CD 2 **21** (CD **2** PLAY ALONG)

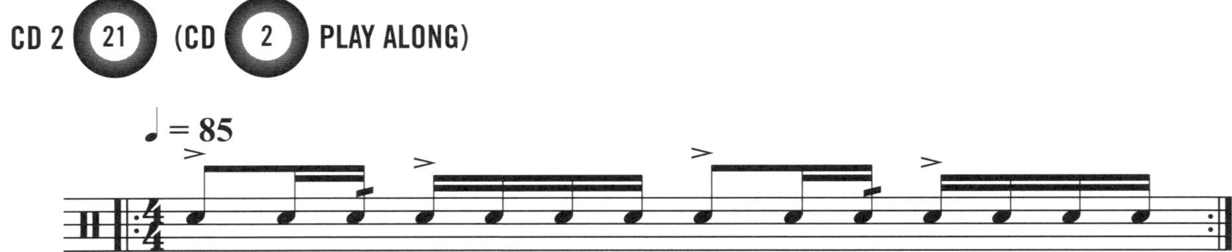

So where are the accents in this Loop?
(Beats 1, 2, 3, and 4)

Therefore, if you played a groove that was based on a very syncopated rhythm, it **would not work well** (or blend) with this loop example.

Notice how the acoustic-drum accents are in direct opposition of the percussion's accent structure.

Therefore, try to play a groove that is based on the downbeat.

Notice how this pattern blends into the percussion's accent structure.

OK, we have now determined that the accents in Loop Example 1 fall on beats 1, 2, 3, and 4.

Fundamental No. 6: What are the pitches of each accent?

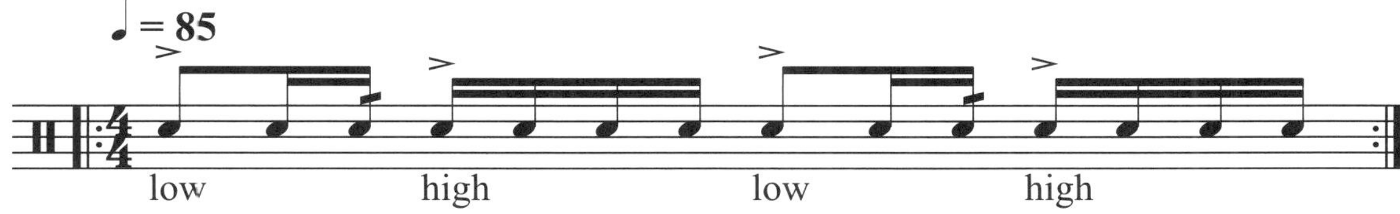

Now we must determine the pitch (or tone) of each accent. For example, is the accent a high-pitched tone or a low- pitched tone? *(Beats 1 and 3 are low pitched and that beats 2 and 4 are high pitched.)*

Fundamental No. 7: Where can you voice those accents on the kit?

Upon examining **Perc. Loop 1 ST,** we determined that the accents were on beats 1, 2, 3 and 4.We also concluded that beats 1 and 3 are low pitched and that beats 2 and 4 are high pitched. These are important characteristics because they will determine where we voice the accent pattern (and then groove) on the drum kit. For example, if there is a low-toned accent,-play a bass drum. Conversely, if there are high-pitched accents, play a snare drum.

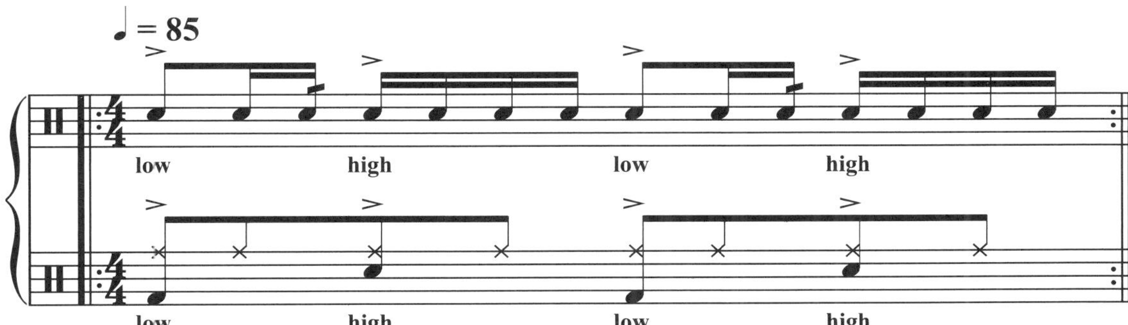

Important Note: the tambourine and shaker amendment for voicing accents
Tambourine and shaker loops maintain the same pitch throughout their accent structure. Therefore, there are two options for voicing their accents on the drumset.

- **Option 1.** You will voice accents that fall on the 1 and 3 side of the beat on the bass drum. Conversely, when voicing accents that fall on the 2 and 4 side of the beat, choose the snare drum.
  Percussion Loop 4

Notation Addition: A diamond-shaped notehead represents a shaker.

CD 2 22   (CD2 26   PLAY ALONG)

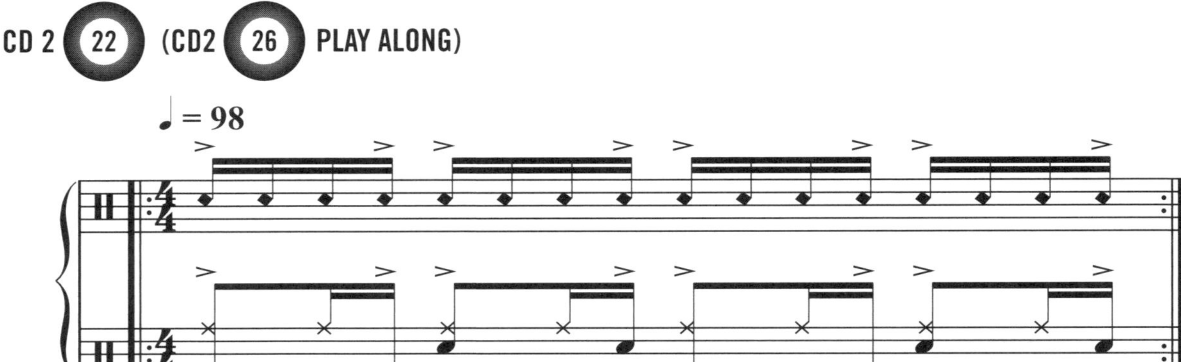

- **Option 2.** Or take a familiar drumset pattern (that also has the same accent structure) and use it along with the percussion loop example:

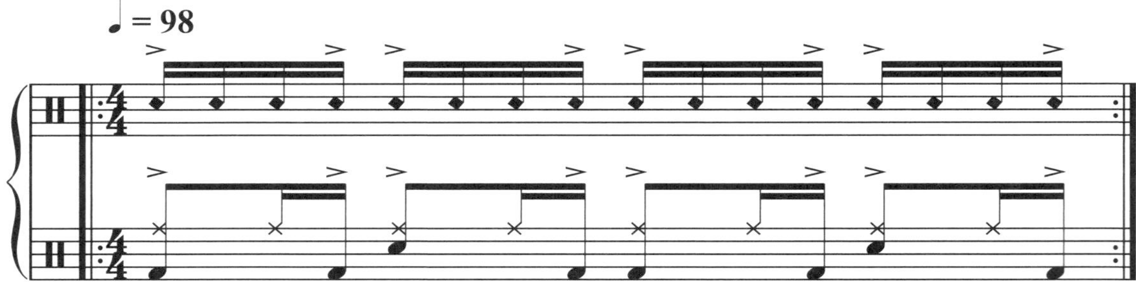

Fundamental No. 8: Are there any holes or rests that you can play between?

The loop figure consists of an eighth note and six sixteenth notes, which repeats twice during the measure. Thus, the entire measure is counted as 1 + a 2 e + a 3 + a 4 e + a.

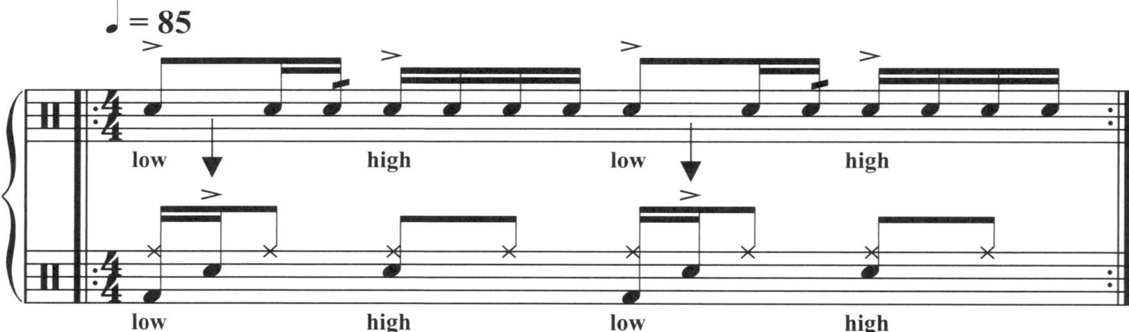

Do you notice how there is a gap between beat 1 and the + of beat 1? (There is nothing happening on the "e" of beat 1). Therefore, it is possible to play in that space and phrase between the loop itself. (Unlike Total Accompaniment, this will not detract from the loop. You must keep in mind that drum loops are used to fatten up a track and give it an unwavering momentum. On the other hand, percussion loops help to generate a particular feel and flavor, rather than a specific drum part.)

Fundamental 5-8 Checklist (For use with each percussion-loop example)

In addition to the Fundamental Four Checklist, you should also xerox this page and place it along side whichever percussion page you are working through in the Book.

5. **Your groove should follow the percussion loop's accent structure.**
   Are the percussion loop's accents on the downbeat, upbeat, or a specific rhythmic figure?

6. **What are the tones of each accent?**
   Determine the pitch of each accent. For example, is the accent a high-pitched tone or a low-pitched tone?

7. **Where can you voice those accents on the Kit?**
   For example, if there is a low-toned accent, play a bass drum. Conversely, if there are high-pitched accents, play a snare drum.

Important Note: Tambourine and shaker Loops maintain the same pitch throughout their accent structure. Therefore, you should voice the accents that fall on the 1 and 3 side of the beat on the bass drum. Conversely, when voicing accents that fall on the 2 and 4 side of the beat, choose the snare drum.

8. **Are there any holes or rests that you can play between?**
   If so, it is possible to play in that space and phrase between the loop itself.

Section 4A: Straight Feel (85–102 bpm Percussion Loops)

Percussion Loop 1

CD 2 (23)

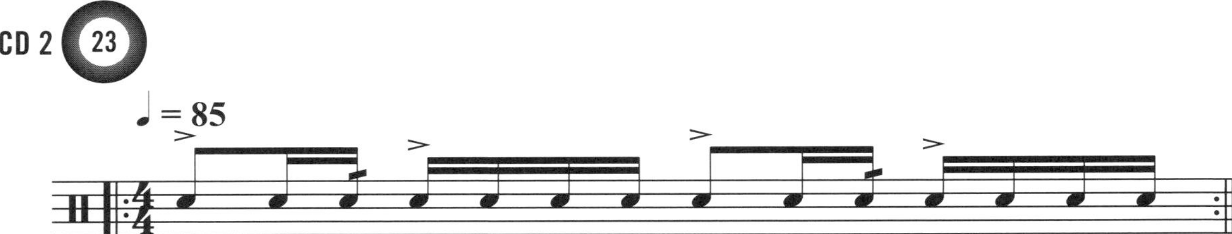

Percussion Loop 2

CD 2 (24)

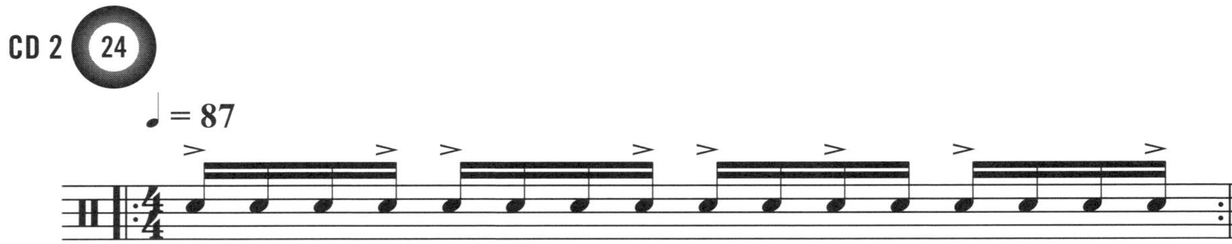

Percussion Loop 3

CD 2 (25)

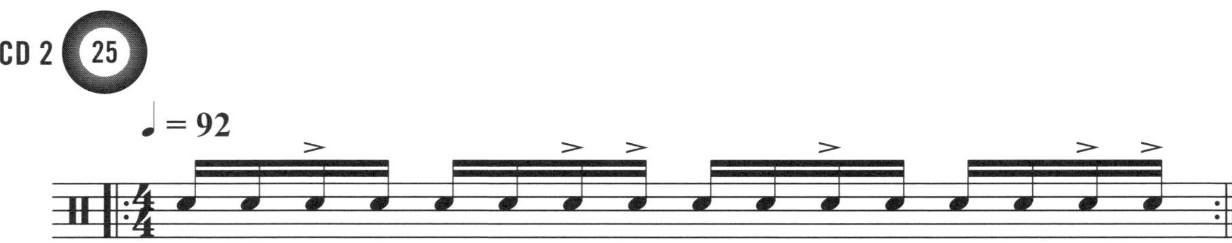

Percussion Loop 4

CD 2 (26)

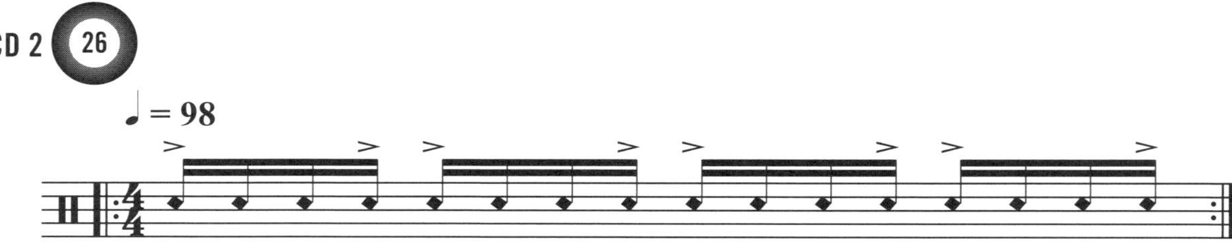

Percussion Loop 5
CD2 Track 27. Play along

Notation Addition: A triangle-shaped note represents a tambourine.

CD 2 (27)

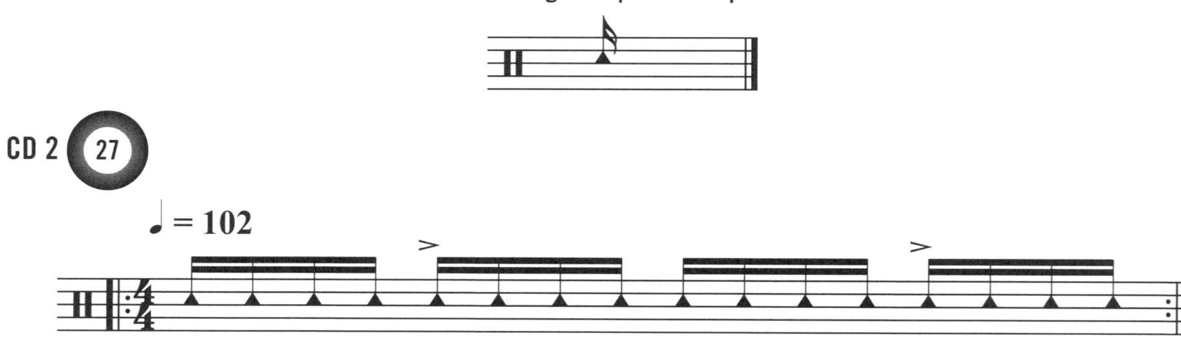

Section 4B: Swing Feel (85–102 bpm Percussion Loops)
Percussion Loop 6

Fundamentals 5–8 Reminder: This Swing-feel Conga pattern has a more "upbeat" feel to it. Thus, the drumset pattern accents a few of the conga's rhythmic accents, again, helping to blend and sound "as one."

CD 2 28

Percussion Loop 7

CD 2 29

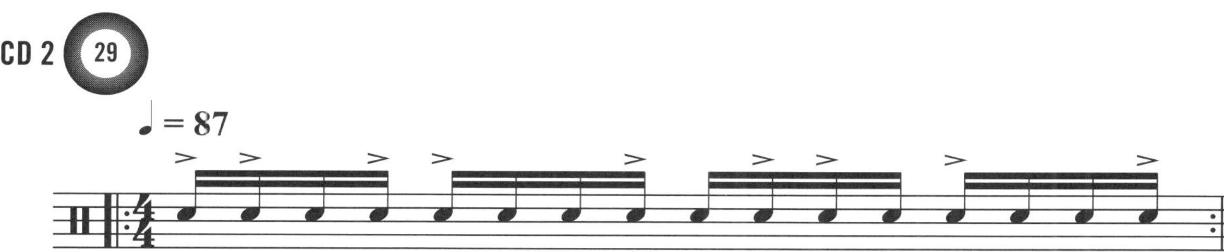

Percussion Loop 8

CD 2 30

Percussion Loop 9

CD 2 31

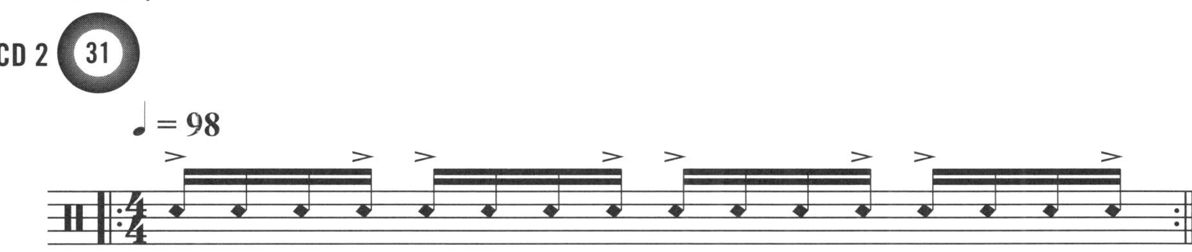

Percussion Loop 10

CD 2 32

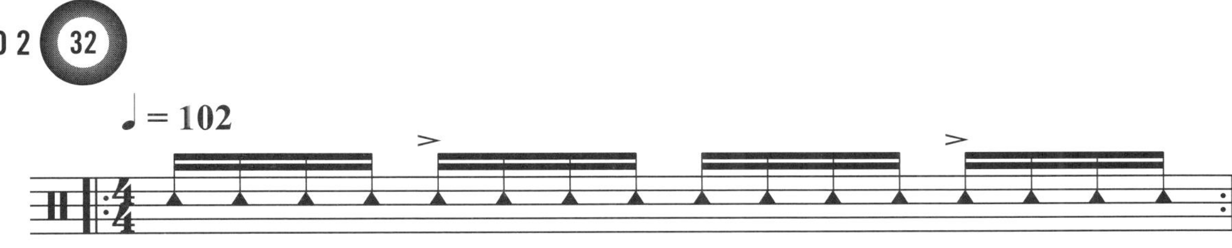

Chapter 5: Instrument Loops

Just as I explained earlier, a click track only provides tempo information. In this chapter on Instrument Loops, the click is used as a "feel" reference point as well. This reference point not only tells us where each instrument loop falls within the beat (ahead, behind or in the middle), but it also is used to aid with count- in, multiple-bar rests (where no instrument is playing), transitions between two different instrument loops and other form-related issues.

This chapter is organized in three sections:
- Rock and Metal Instrument Loops.
- Pop Rock Instrument Loops.
- Hip Hop Instrument Loops.

All of the loops in this chapter are combined into full Backing Tracks in Chapter 6 (p. 71).

Total Accompaniment Reminder:
Play within the Feel of the Instrument Loop (Not just the Click Track)

It is not enough to simply lock in with the click track. You must also play within the feel of the instrument loop as well. For instance, if the loop is behind the beat, you must play behind the beat too. The audience will hear each instrument loop, but they will not hear the click track!

So how can you learn to groove with an instrument loop that is not exactly with the click track? Well, let's listen to the bass line from

Pop Inst Loop 6 (CD2 **43** Play Along)

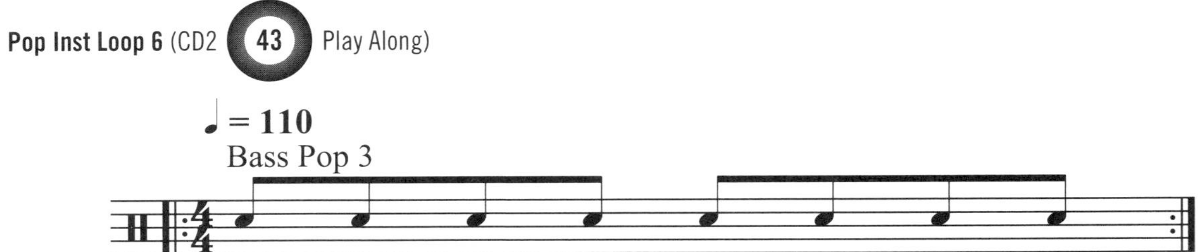

Do you notice how this bass line is extremely on top of the beat? Therefore, if you are only lining up with the click track, you will sound "off" from the bass and its groove.

So here is the solution: You must play more toward the bass loop (instead of the click track). For example:

CD 2 33

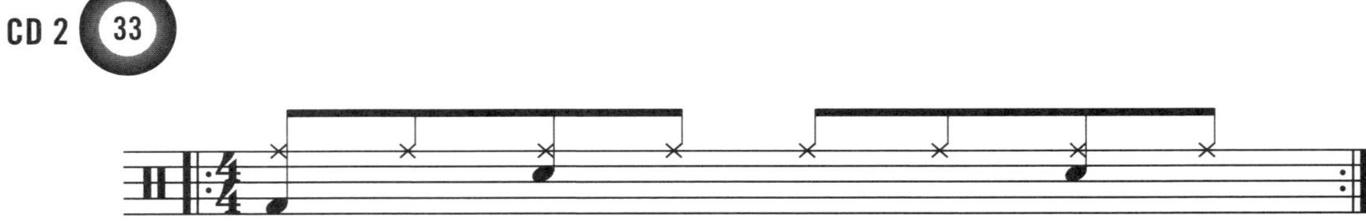

Do you notice how this approach camouflages the imperfections of the bass loop? Therefore, the cumulative groove works better and grooves harder.

Rock and Metal Backing Track 1: Individual Loop Phrases

Rock and Metal Inst. Loop 1

CD 2 34

Rock and Metal Inst. Loop 2

CD 2 35

Rock and Metal Backing Track 2: Individual Loop Phrases

Rock and Metal Inst. Loop 3

CD 2 36

Rock and Metal Backing Track 3: Individual Loop Phrases

Rock and Metal Inst. Loop 4

CD 2 37

Pop Rock Backing Track 1: Individual Loop Phrases

Pop Rock Inst. Loop 1

CD 2 (38)

Pop Rock Inst. Loop 2

CD 2 (39)

Pop Rock Backing Track 2: Individual Loop Phrases

Pop Rock Inst. Loop 3

CD 2 (40)

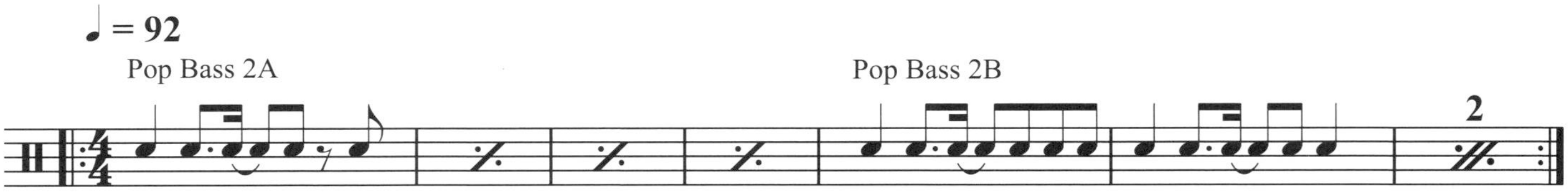

Pop Rock Inst. Loop 4

CD 2 (41)

Pop Rock Inst. Loop 5

CD 2 (42)

Pop Rock Backing Track 3: Individual Loops

Pop Rock Inst. Loop 6

CD 2 43

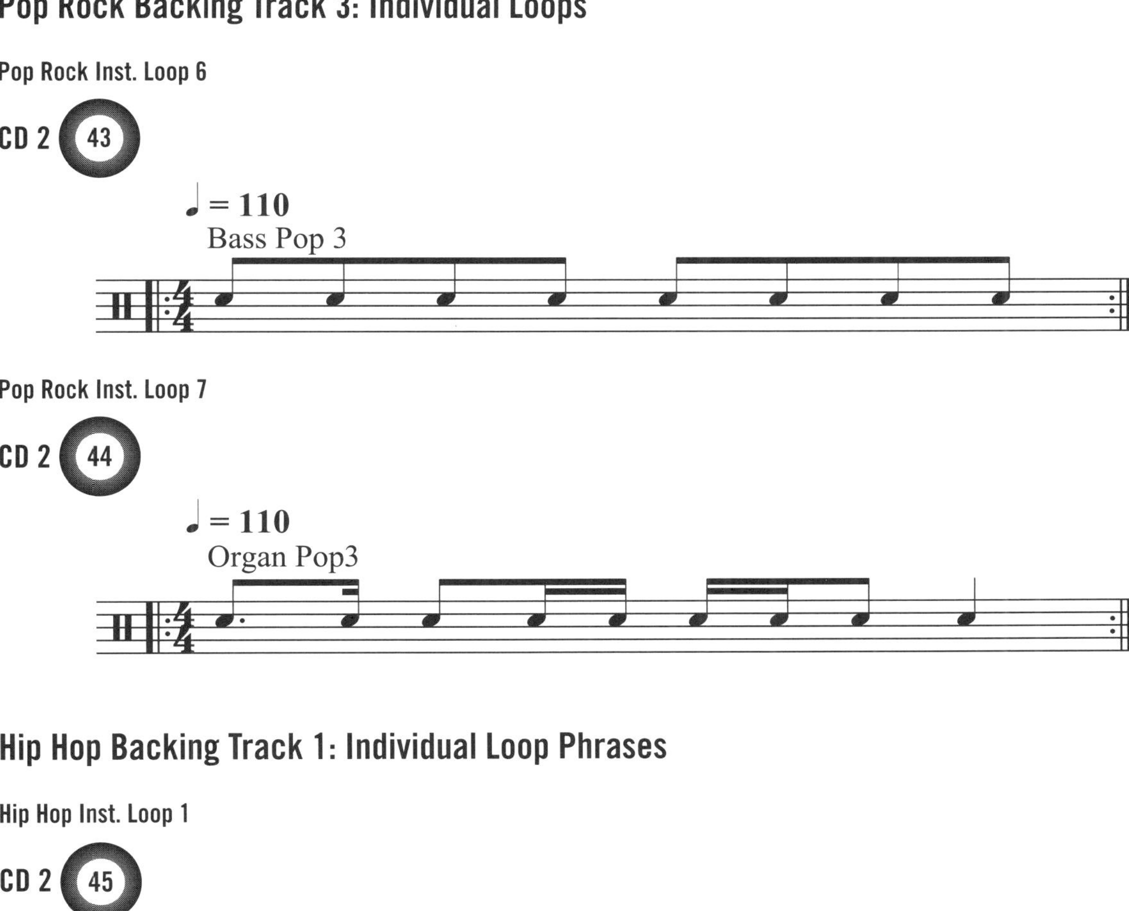

Pop Rock Inst. Loop 7

CD 2 44

Hip Hop Backing Track 1: Individual Loop Phrases

Hip Hop Inst. Loop 1

CD 2 45

♩ = 85

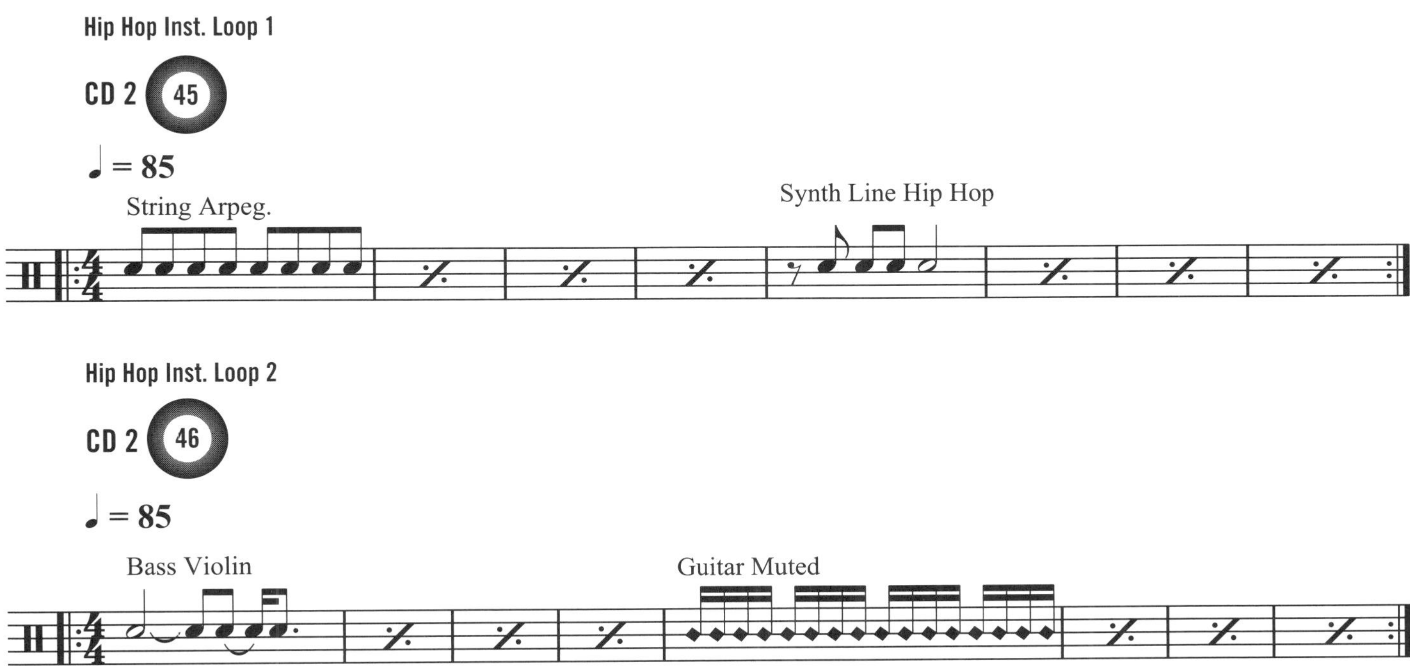

Hip Hop Inst. Loop 2

CD 2 46

♩ = 85

Hip Hop Backing Track 2: Individual Loop Phrases

Hip Hop Inst. Loop 3

CD 2 47

♩ = 90

Hip Hop Inst. Loop 4

CD 2 **48**

♩ = 90

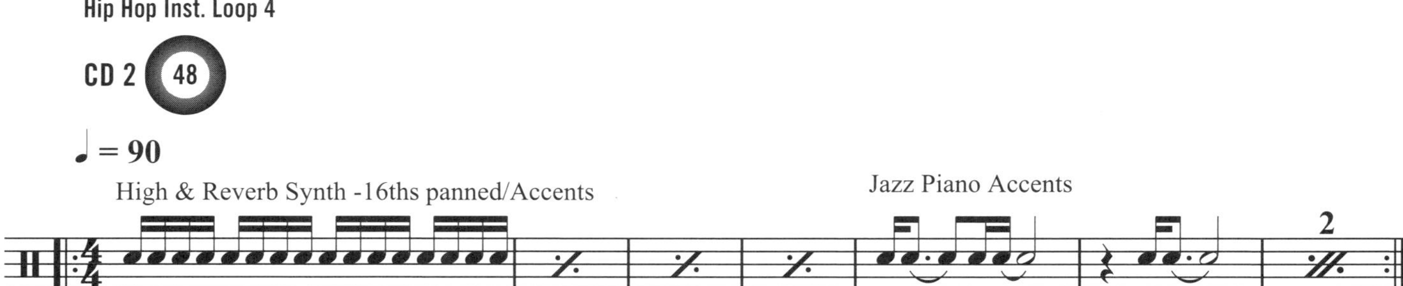

Hip Hop Backing Track 3: Individual Loop Phrases

Hip Hop Inst. Loop 5

CD 2 **49**

♩ = 75

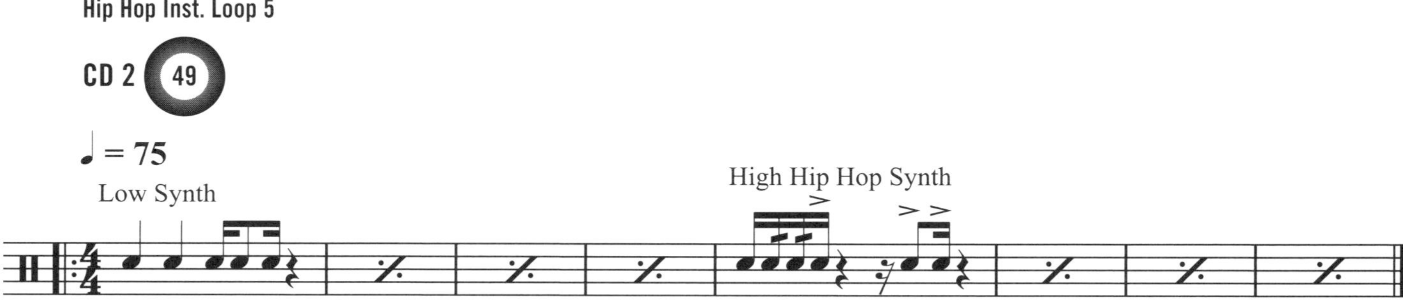

Total Accompaniment:
An Additional Practice Loop

Timed Sound FX (Effects)
(With a Click Track)

However, there are still moments when using a traditional click track is appropriate. Many jingle sessions, film scores and live gigs utilize a click track to help keep you in time with the other sonic landscapes that jump sporadically in and out of a track. There could be voices, one-bar Loops, or crazy sounds that are "in time", but do not occur every measure (This is where a click really helps out).

It is also important that you do not get distracted by the Sound FX themselves and consequently lose the groove. With time, you will get used to syncing with a click and STILL grooving with the other sounds that are rhythmically present in the mix.

FX Loop Practice Track

In this FX Loop Practice Track, there are two bars of click, followed by two bars of various Sound FX that fade in and out of the track. Have fun!

CD 2 **50**

♩ = 120

Chapter 6: Backing Tracks

This method combines *all* four of the previous concepts (Drum Loops, Percussion Loops, Instrument Loops, and FX Loops), and it is also the most challenging aspect of performing with loops.

Nowadays, when you are called upon to work on a track in the studio, you are usually the first (or sometimes only) live instrument to be recorded. Up until that point most composers write exclusively with MIDI Instruments and Drum Loops of *all* types. Not only is this method cheaper than the days of demo recording, but it allows the composer to point the musicians toward their artistic vision without a player's style coloring the composition.

When these sessions occur, you are typically asked to play with an existing programmed drum track (or loop) and add the feel and tone of live drums as well. This is extremely difficult because not only do you have to play (and groove) with the synthetic drum track present, you also have to become one with the feel of the bass loop, guitar loop and every other sound present.

In the following pages there are combinations of all the previous loop examples. Each subsection of drum loops, instrument loops and FX loops are combined into full backing tracks for you to play along with; *so treat them like real sessions and get to work!*

This chapter is organized in three sections:
• Rock and Metal Backing Tracks
• Pop Rock Backing Tracks
• Hip Hop Backing Tracks

Rock and Metal Backing Track 1

Instrument Loops = Rock and Metal Inst. Loops 1 and 2
Drum Loops = Rock and Metal Loops 4, 5, and 5a

Notation Reminder: Multiple Bar Repeat

In this chart, the multiple-bar repeat signifies that you will play five more bars of the previous groove. The others indicate to repeat the previous two measures.

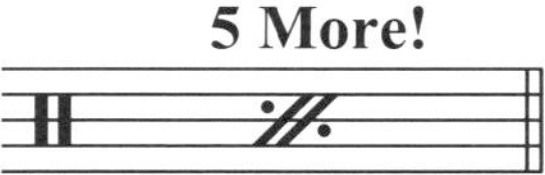

Rock and Metal Backing Track 2

Instrument Loops = Rock and Metal Inst. Loop 3
Drum Loops = Rock and Metal Loops 7a and 8a
FX Loops = Metal FX Loop 5

CD 2 **52**

Rock and Metal Backing Track 3

Instrument Loops = Rock and Metal Inst. Loop 4
Drum Loops = Rock and Metal Loop 2a
FX Loops = Metal FX Loop 4

Notice how the A sections grooves are not notated. Use your ears and come up with a backbeat groove that works!

$\quad = 120$

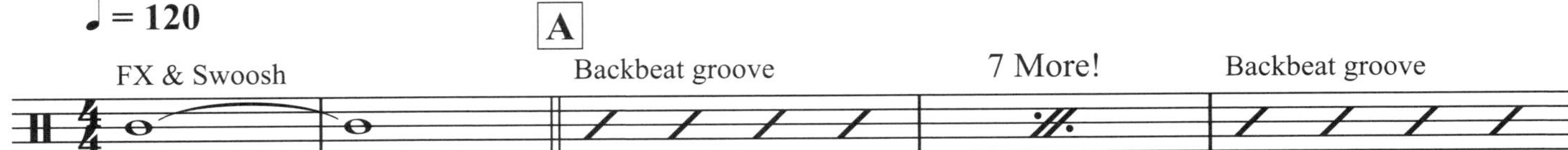

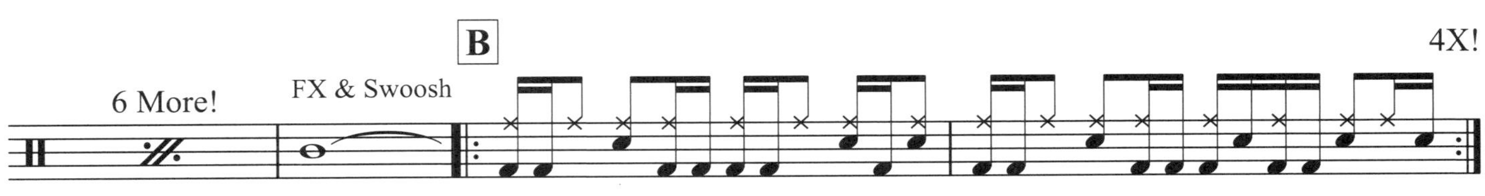

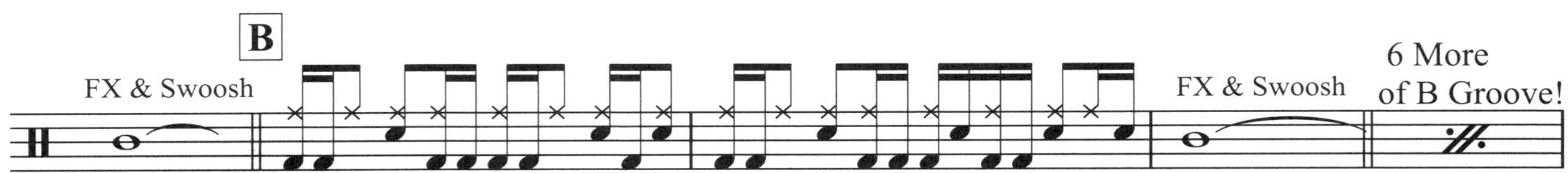

Pop Rock Backing Track 1

Instrument Loops = Pop Rock Inst. Loops 1& 2
Drum Loops = Pop Rock 2a
FX Loops = none
Percussion Loop = Loop 1

♩ = **80**

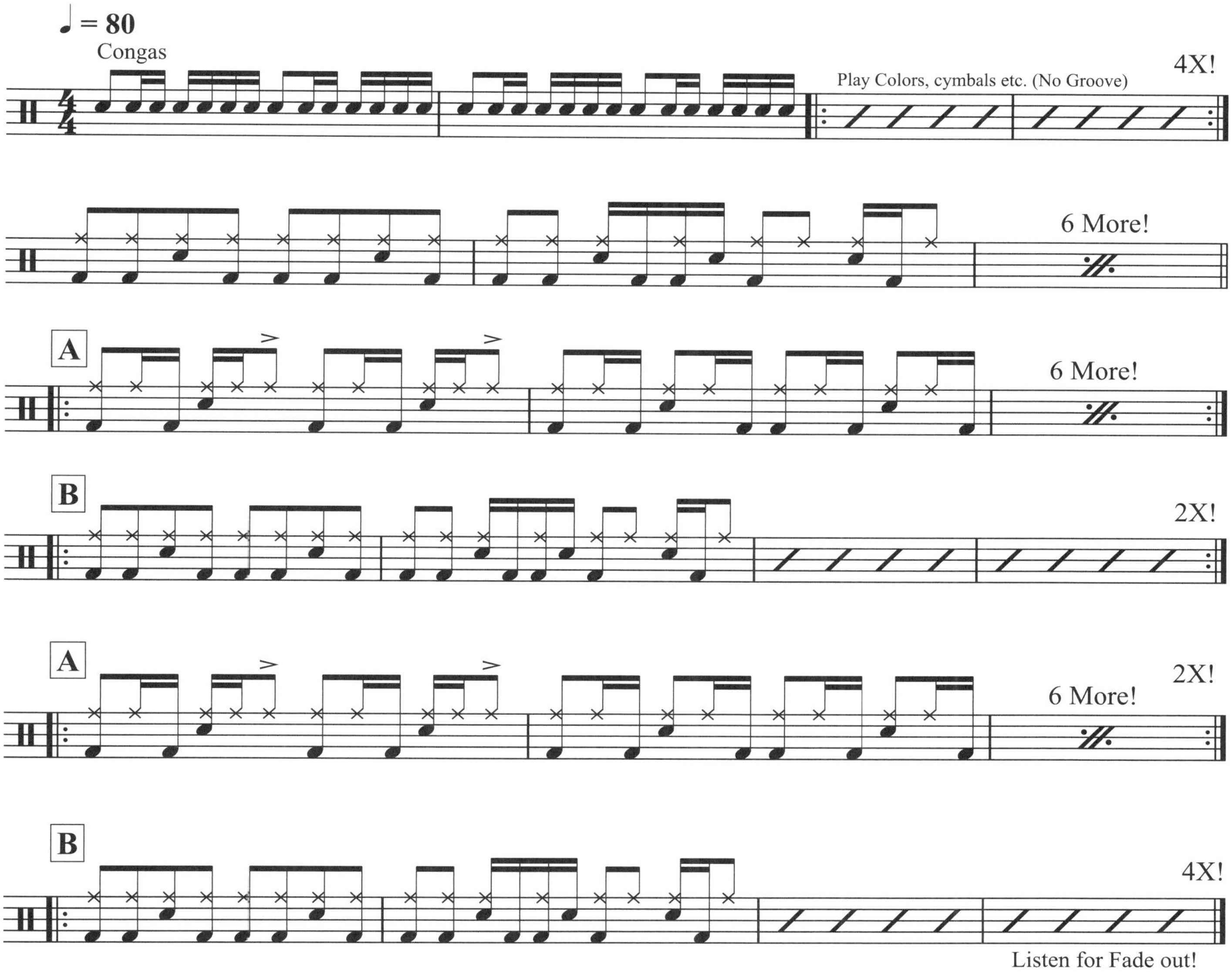

Pop Rock Backing Track 2

Instrument Loops = Pop Rock Inst. Loops 3, 4, & 5,
Drum Loops = Pop Rock 13a and 6a
FX Loops = Wooooooooosh!

CD 2  55

Pop Rock Backing Track 3

Instrument Loops = Pop Rock Inst. Loops 6 & 7
Drum Loops = Total Accompaniment Loop Example Tracks 1 and 2

Notation Addition: Bar

On the last line (staff) of this solo, there is a single $\frac{2}{4}$ bar. Therefore, when you reach this measure, count (and play) for two beats and then return to $\frac{4}{4}$ time.

CD 2 56

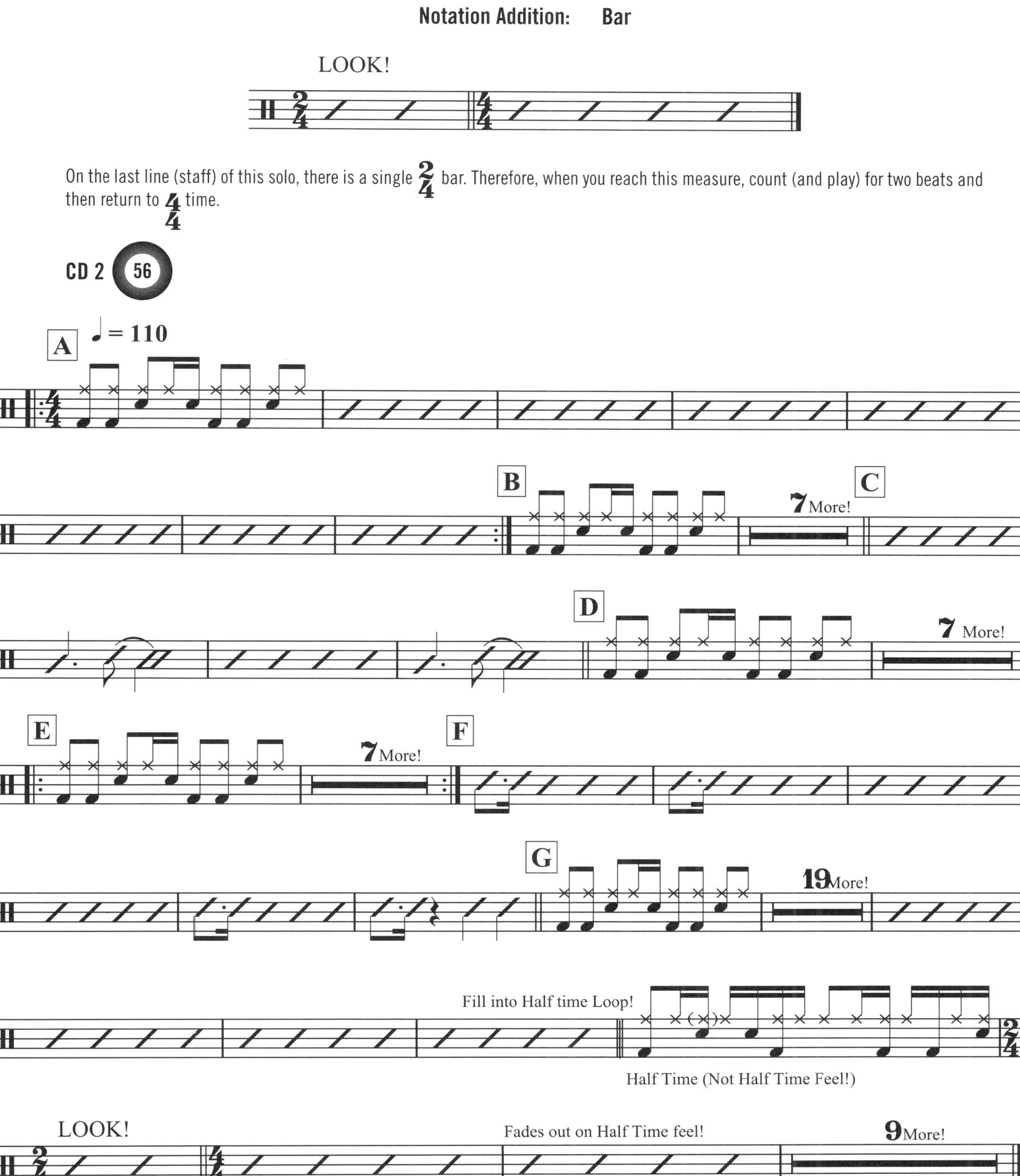

Half-time feel, not half time!

Hip Hop Backing Track 1
Instrument Loops = Hip Hop Inst. Loops 1 & 2
Drum Loops = Loops 1 & 3 (Section 3A)

Notation Reminder: D.C. al Fine

D.C. signifies that you must return to the beginning of the chart. Furthermore, *Fine* is a musical term for end. Thus, you will return to the beginning of the chart (D.C.) and end when you see the term *Fine.*

Notation Reminder: Rehearsal Letters

Notice that this solo contains two distinct sections: an "A" section and a "B" section. Each letter represents a new idea and melodic motif.

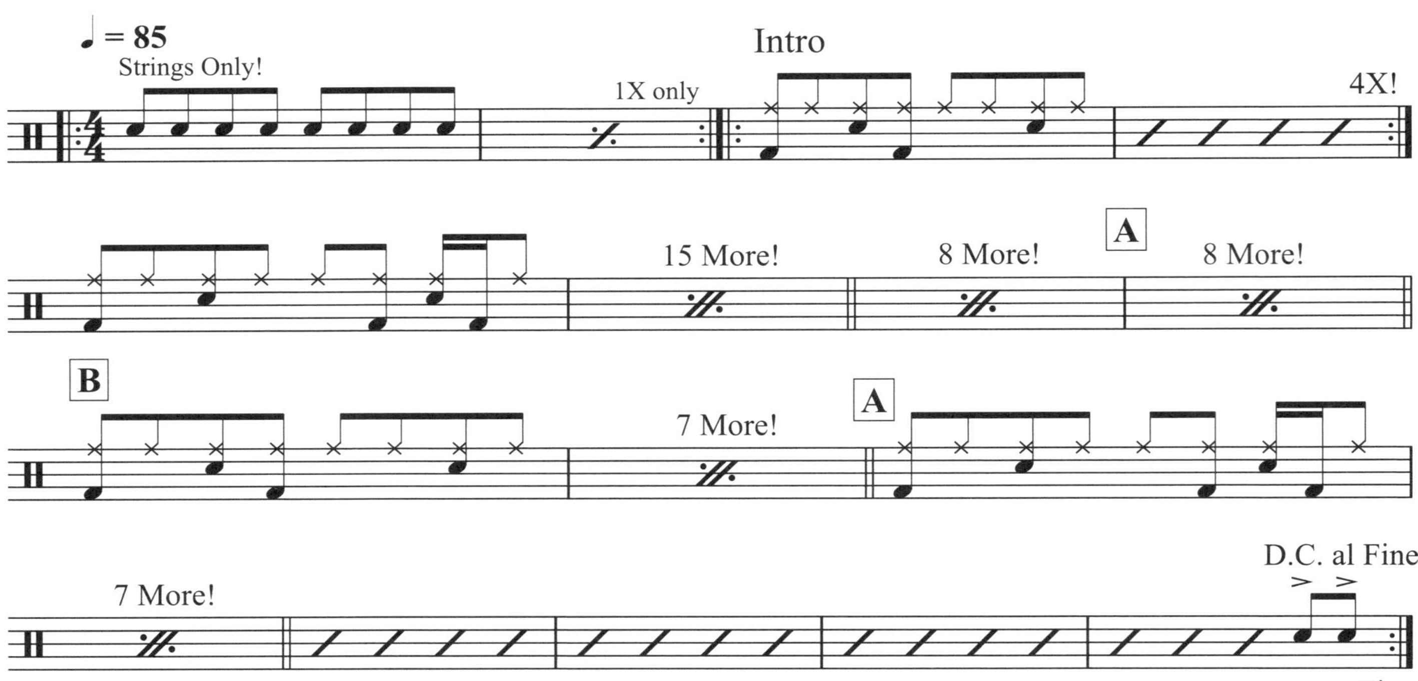

Hip Hop Backing Track 2

Instrument Loops = Hip Hop Inst. Loops 3 & 4
Drum Loops = New Loop for this Chart
FX Loops = None

Hip Hop Broken Feels Backing Track 3

Instrument Loops = Hip Hop Inst. Loop 5
Drum Loops = Hip Hop Loop 22

Music Addition: Hip Hop Loop 22 has been modified into a 2 Bar Phrase

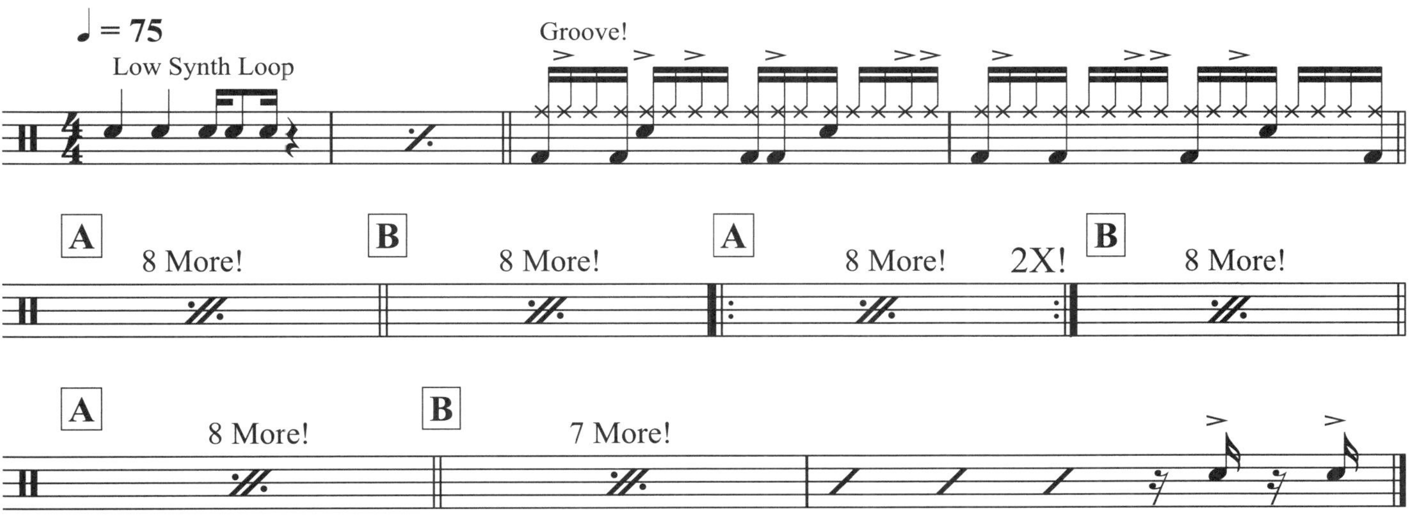

Part 3: Appendices

This seven part section will take you through the very basics of terminology, the various hardware/software devices (and their function), help you build a live rig from the ground up, and describe a typical real world working scenario as well. In addition, there is a list of supplemental drum-related texts.

In time, you will have the tools to understand and integrate the vast world of sample-based music into your Drumming repertoire.

Appendix A: Vocabulary

In order to communicate and maneuver in this electronic world, you will need to learn some very specific vocabulary. These terms will range from the very basic to extremely specific; don't be intimidated! Once you comprehend these basic building blocks, you will be well on your way to fully understanding what is needed to accomplish *the goal.*

Basic Terms
- **Playing with a Click.** Basic term that refers to the use of a metronome. A click is used to synchronize you with other elements while recording or playing live.
- **Sample.** A digital recording / "Snippet" of any sound, groove or musical tone.
- **Loop.** A repeated portion of a sample that creates a sustaining sound, usually a one- or two-bar drum groove.
- **Loop Fragment.** A portion of the original two- or four-bar loop used as an accent.
- **MIDI (Musical Instrument Digital Interface).** A digital language that allows multiple electronic instruments, computers and other related devices to communicate within a connected network. It operates on the premise that each musical note, dynamic, or quality corresponds to a number. For example, C is 36, C # is 37, D is 38 etc. MIDI volume 0–127 etc. Note: MIDI does *not* record audio or sound. It records information.
- **Sequence.** MIDI data that is recorded and/or played back. It is very similar to a paper roll on a player piano. (numbers/holes on a piano roll).
- **Triggering.** MIDI events played live. For drummers this usually means striking a pad that "triggers" a MIDI note number to be played. For example, you strike a pad that is programmed to MIDI number 36 (striking the pad triggers/plays a C Note).
- **Programmed Drum Tracks.** Drum beats that are played or programmed into a MIDI sequencer or drum machine (Synthesized Drums). Most early 80s records had programmed drum tracks that were done on the classic synthesizers of the day.
- **WAV File.** A type of audio file that is used on both Macintosh and PC platforms. WAVs can be full songs, samples or loops.
- **AIFF File.** An audio file associated with the Macintosh platform. They can be full songs, loops or samples.
- **Digital Audio.** A recording that is digitized.
- **Compression.** The use of a compressor while recording. "Compressed". See "Compressor" in Equipment Terms.

Equipment Terms
- **Sequencer.** A device that records and plays back a series of MIDI events. It is very similar to a recordable player piano. It does not record audio; but it does record information (such as, note numbers). They can be:
1. Hardware-based: A machine that is built and used specifically designed to be a sequencer.
2. Software-based: A software sequencing program that runs on a computer. (Some people prefer this option because they already own a computer).
- **Drum Machine.** A simple sequencer that specializes in drum sounds and sequences only drum patterns.
- **Sampler.** A type of synthesizer which derives its sounds from recording audio (instruments or non-musical sounds) and then stores them in computer memory, either on floppy disc, hard drive, or onto CDR. They are used extensively for generating sound effects. Like a sequencer, samplers can be both Hardware and software based.
- **Trigger interface.** A device that converts drum hits into MIDI information. This information is translated into specific sounds and qualities. A few good examples are Roland's V Drum, Clavia's Ddrum and Yamahas DTX Series Modules. Playing a drum pad sends the MIDI data to the module and coverts that information into sound.
- **Mixer.** A device which combines many different audio signals together and outputs them in mono or stereo. They come in many sizes and are referred to by the number of channels (different audio inputs) they have.
- **Direct Box (DI).** A small box that takes a 1/4 inch (unbalanced) input and converts it to an XLR (balanced) output. Usually, this is needed to send a balanced signal to the main mixing console.

- **In-Ear Monitors.** Small headphones that are placed in your ear, that allow you to monitor mixes and various other sound sources, without the large look and extreme isolation of clunky headphones.
- **Power Conditioner.** A advanced version of a power strip. It has multiple inputs for electronic devices, and it shields these devices from power surges or irregular power currents.
- **Mini disc Player.** A deck that is essentially an advanced audio tape recorder. The sound is stored on a disc that is small in size. These discs do not skip (at all), and they have the same audio quality as a CD.
- **Rack Case.** A case that holds many different types of audio, MIDI and electronic gear. They are 19" wide, and the devices are held in place by four screws (two on each rack ear). In addition, most companies design their equipment to fit these cases.
- **Soft Synths.** Software Synthesizers. They are drum machines, samplers and synthesizers in software (rather than hardware) form.
- **Compressor.** A compressor is a specialized amplifier used to reduce the dynamic range span between the softest and loudest sounds. It achieves a more uniform, more consistent audio signal that is optimum for some styles of music.

Appendix B: Working Method Concepts

Now that you understand the basic concepts and terminology, where do you go from here? How will you build a rig and integrate these elements into your playing? A lot will depend on your goals. For instance, do you want to trigger sampled sound effects from pads, perform to predetermined/recorded sequences, or trigger loops and loop fragments live? Here are some of the more important factors to consider when determining which working method(s) are right for you:

- **Triggering various samples and sound FX** within your show is by far the simplest to accomplish. This is because most sound effects are "not timed," and therefore, a click track will not be needed to sync up with them. As far as gear, all you will need is a sampler and a trigger interface.
- **Performing to predetermined sequences** is a slightly different predicament. It requires some precision and rehearsal. Since the music you will be playing to has a set form and structure (i.e., it is prerecorded), you will need to play with a click track and memorize the various sections of each song. This method is similar to playing with your favorite CD, although after the initial rehearsing this method sounds extremely full and it is very low maintenance. (All you will have to do is play your acoustic kit to the backing track.) You will need a sequencer, sampler, in ear monitors, and a mixer.
- **Manually triggering loops and loop fragments live** is by far the most labor-intensive method of performing. Essentially, you will trigger (or play) every single loop, loop fragment and sample that is present in a song. This can be technically difficult (although not impossible) to do while grooving on an acoustic kit. You will be required not only to groove hard and sync up with the timed loops, but you will also be responsible for every direction taken in the song. On the positive side, this method of working allows for the most improvisation; there is no set structure. You will need a sampler, trigger interface, trigger pads, in ear monitors/headphones, and a click.

Your preferred working method will determine the complexity of your setup (the equipment needed), your overall monetary investment, and, most importantly, the direction of your performances. **So be realistic and choose your goals wisely.**

Using electronics in conjunction with acoustic drumming can be an extremely adventurous and rewarding experience. After playing with loops and click tracks on a nightly basis, your drumming will grow exponentially. You will groove harder, become more fluent in electronic-based music, and be more sensitive to song forms and structure.

Appendix C: In-Depth Working Methods

In the last few pages, we discussed the basic vocabulary needed to maneuver in the electronic world and the three technical working methods (triggering sound FX, playing to prerecorded sequences, and manually triggering all timed elements to a click track) available to achieve our goals. Now we have these basic concepts under our belt, we can take what we have learned and develop it into a live working rig and situation.

Triggering Various Samples and Sound FX

As stated in the last section, triggering various samples and sound FX within your playing is by far the simplest to accomplish. This is because most sound FX are "not timed," and therefore, a click track will *not* be needed to sync up with them.

Scenario 1

We will begin with a fundamental setup that includes a trigger interface and a drum machine. (Make sure that your MIDI cable is connected from the MIDI OUT of the trigger interface into the MIDI IN of your drum machine.)

First, we need to assign a MIDI channel to both your trigger interface and sound source. MIDI channels are essentially addresses, and in order for each device to communicate with one other, they need to be set to the same address/MIDI Channel. (There are 16 different MIDI channels/addresses available, and each is usually used to connect your interface to a different sound source.) In this case we only have one sound source, so set your trigger interface to **send** on MIDI channel 1 and your drum machine to **receive** on MIDI channel 1.

Secondly, we must select the drum samples that we want to use and find out their corresponding MIDI note numbers. (Remember, MIDI operates on the premise that each musical note or sample corresponds to a number). For now let's choose drum samples with familiar tones such as a bass drum, snare and closed hi-hat and assume that they are in GM (General MIDI) format. Example: bass drum is No. 36, Snare is No. 38 and closed hi-hat is No. 42.

Electronic-instrument manufacturers agreed to a worldwide standard layout for certain specified Sounds; they called this the General MIDI (GM) standard. Here is the General MIDI drum layout present on most modern drum machines manufactured today. **C2-36** reads as C (pitch on the piano), 2 (second octave on the piano) and 36 MIDI note number.

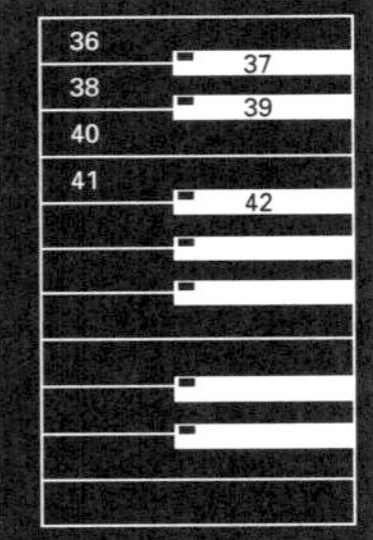

General MIDI (Partial) Drum Layout

C2-36: Bass Drum
C # 2-37: Side Stick
D2-38: Snare
D #2-39: Clap
E2-40: Elec. Snare
F2-41: Low Tom
F #2-42: Closed hi-hat

Thirdly, let's go into the edit/assign menu of our trigger interface (such as a DrumKat) and match your pad of choice with the corresponding MIDI number (i.e., drum sample). Now assign pad 1 to MIDI note number 38/Snare. Now when you hit pad 1, you should hear your sound source's snare sound.

Example: Pad1 = MIDI Note D2=38

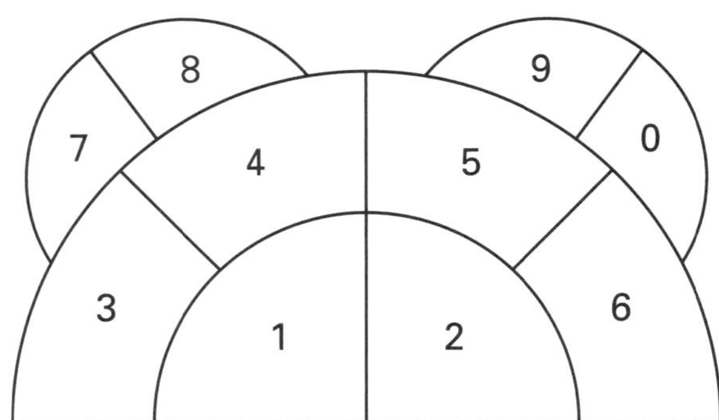

Scenario 2

This set up almost identical to the last, except that in this case, the drum machine is replaced by a digital sampler or laptop with a soft synth/sampler package. (Remember, a sampler is type of synthesizer which derives its samples from digitally recording sounds and then storing them in computer memory.) There are three major differences between the drum machine and our new sampler scenario. This setup is not limited by the sounds present inside a factory preset device. We may now (1) create/record custom samples from any source, (2) assign our custom-made samples to custom note numbers (straying from the General MIDI layout) and (3) create patches/programs that have more detail than a normal drum machine by including multiple samples of each particular sound.

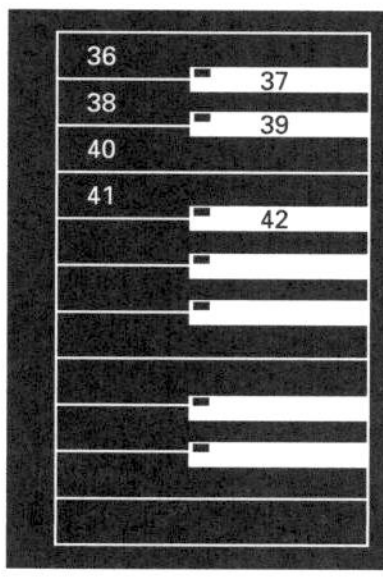

Custom Drum Layout

C2-36: Scream voice
C #2-37: Bass Woofer
D2-38: Electric Snare
D #2-39: Cabassa
E2-40: Bass Drum
F2-41: Car Horn
F #2-42: EFX hi-hat

Performing to pre-determined sequences

This section is going to assume that you already have working knowledge of a basic drum machine and how to operate it. This method is similar to playing with your favorite CD, although (after the initial rehearsing) this method sounds extremely full and it is very low maintenance. All you have to do is play to the prerecorded tracks.

Simple Sequence

This working method builds upon the previous drum machine scenario. You are essentially going to program a drum machine pattern/beat and play with it (while on your acoustic kit). This drum machine beat is basically a stripped down-simple version of a prerecorded backing track.

Example: While in **4/4**, program bass drum (MIDI No. 36) on beat 1 and the "&" of beat 2, snare (MIDI No. 38) on beats 2 and 4, and closed hi-hat (MIDI No. 42) on all eighth notes.

Complex Sequence

In this instance you are going to take the *Simple Sequence* ideology a couple steps further and add not only another groove/section to the prerecorded sequence; but a couple of one-measure rests too. Since the Music you will be playing to has a set form (i.e., it is prerecorded) *and* measures of rest, you will need to play with (and program) a click track.

Remember the preceding Simple Sequence example? Play/program the previous groove for seven bars; the eighth measure will be a one-measure rest with a quarter-note click playing.

Programming 1

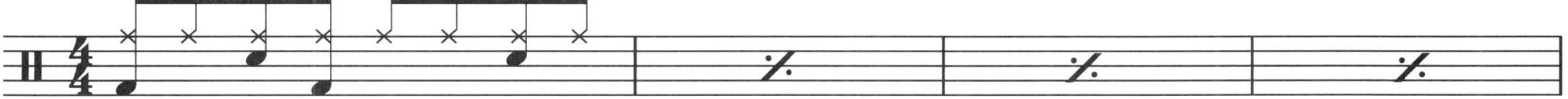

Now create a new pattern with the bass drum on beat 1and the "&" of beat 3, the snare on beats 2 and 4, and closed hi-hat on all eighth notes. Then add an open hi-hat on beat 1.

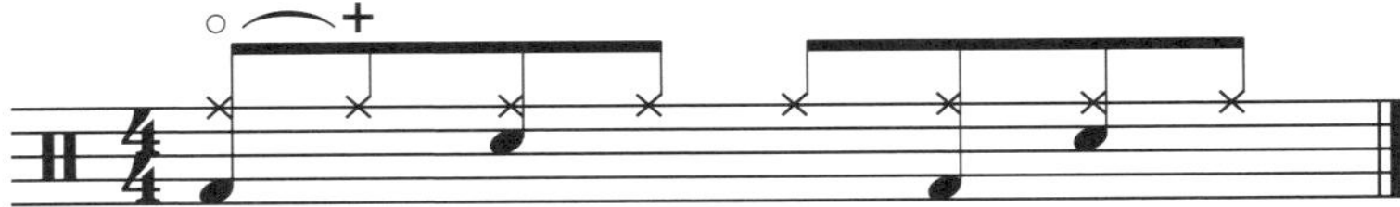

Then put it into another eight-bar format, seven bars of the new groove and one bar of rest with the click.

Programming 2

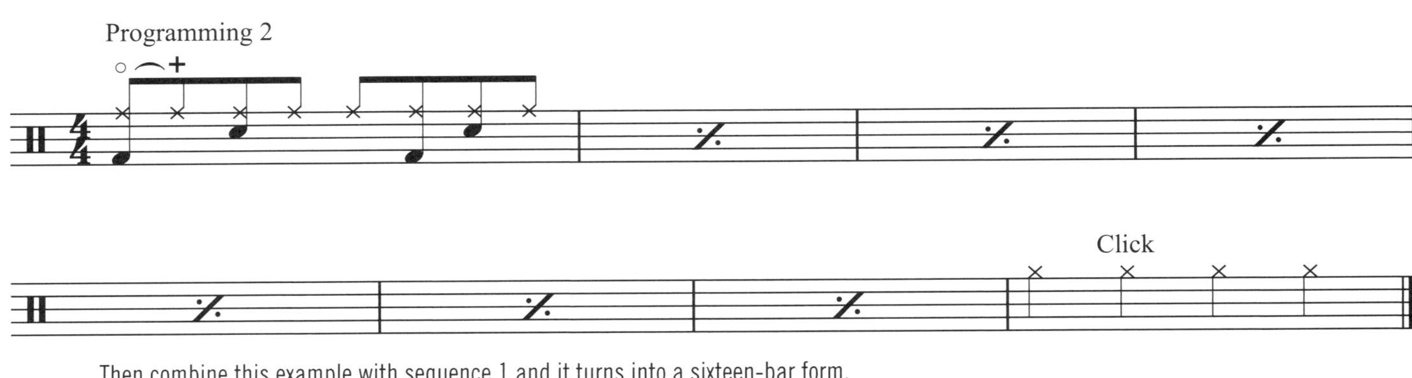

Then combine this example with sequence 1 and it turns into a sixteen-bar form.

Programming 1

Programming 2

Now, once you add other instruments to this with a Digital Audio Workstation (DAW) or Soft Synth, this example is *starting* to resemble a "real-life" backing track that has sections and transitions, which you might accompany on a gig. (You can even combine this method of working with the previous *Triggering Sounds* methods.)

Easy Option
Another option (so that you can either free up your drum machine memory or not bring it to the gig at all) is recording your music onto a DAT machine or Mini-disc Recorder. Both of these formats are extremely reliable (they will not skip during stage vibrations), and the only thing you need to do, besides groove to the tracks, is press play!

Manually Triggering Loops and Loop Fragments

With this strategy, you will also be responsible for triggering (playing) each and every loop in addition to grooving with each. On the positive side, this technique allows for the most improvisation, as there is no set structure.

This system incorporates some elements that are present in each of the previous working methods. Thus, you will still need to:
• Assign a MIDI channel to both your trigger interface and sampler.
• Select (and/or record) the drum loops that you want to use.
• Assign them to MIDI note numbers.
• Enter the edit/assign menu of our trigger interface.
• Match your pad of choice with the corresponding MIDI note number of each drum loop.

However, because each loop/sample you will be triggering is at a *specific tempo*, you will also need to have a click track running to keep you in sync with these timed elements. (Your click can be generated from a metronome, drum machine, or a DAT/Mini-disc Recorder).

Example: Let's assume that your loops are at 90 bpm. Start your click at 90 bpm and groove. Now, trigger your timed loops that are also at 90; YOU WILL BE in sync with them. This is the concept!

Dealing with the Click: P.A. Issues

Alright, we now comprehend how to work, create, and play within each of the three methods. The next major hurdle deals with how to send our sounds/loops/grooves to the House P.A. system *without* the audience hearing the click track.

The theory is relatively simple. Any stereo drum machine, sampler, or DAT/Mini-disc Recorder is essentially a two-track entity. There is a right channel and a left channel to the stereo field, and we can use this to our advantage. While you work with any of the sounds/samples/loops, always pan them to the left channel in the stereo field. While you work with the click track, always assign it to the right channel of the stereo field. Then when it is time to send your signal to the House P.A.: **only send the left (loop) channel.** Now you will be the only person to hear the click track because it is on the right side (channel) of your headphone's stereo mix, and it is not being sent to the House P.A. system. (Thus, your loops will be in your left earphone and the click in your right one).

Appendix D: My Setup

In the last few sections, we have discussed not only the basic vocabulary of loop-based music, but also the technical working methods available as well. Now let's take a look at the assorted equipment setups that I use along with the previously mentioned working methods.

A Note on this Section

Again, this section is written from a commercial, mainstream and popular viewpoint. Consequently, the equipment setups presented within this section focus entirely on fulfilling the requirements in most Pop music, Hip Hop and Rock-band settings. However, I do realize that there are electronic drumset musicians such as Akira Jimbo and Tony Verderosa that perform with more complicated setups in both a solo capacity and group-performance setting.

Setup 1: A Mini-disc Recorder and a Line Mixer for Performing to Predetermined Sequences

Since many artists that I work with have songs that are set in form and length, I use this setup for the majority of my live work. Not only does this equipment configuration enable me to concentrate fully on my acoustic-drum performance (rather than on a wide variety of technical issues such as calling up various patches on my laptop and triggering loops in real time), but it is also extremely road-worthy and requires very little set-up (and tear-down) time on gigs. Furthermore, it is the foundation of my more complex rigs as well.

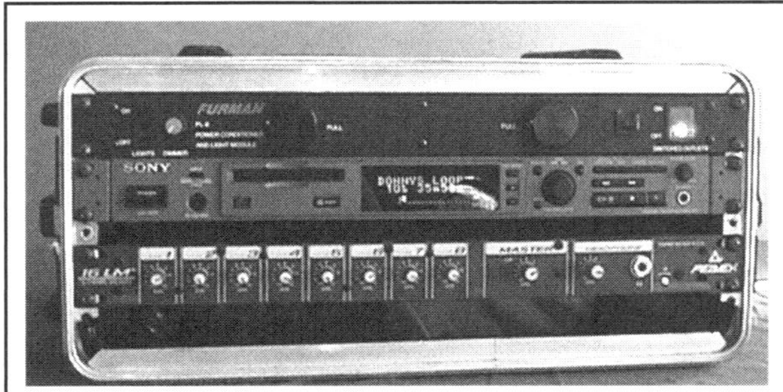 

Figure 1: A Full Rackmount Solution

In this four-space rack case, I have the following items (from top to bottom):
- **A Power Conditioner.** This item provides the AC power to my gear and protects them from power surges as well.
- **Rackmount Mini-disc Recorder.** This item provides the loops and backing tracks. (The loops are recorded to the left channel and the Click is recorded to the Right Channel).
- **8-Channel Line Mixer.** The mixer acts as my own personal headphone-monitoring system with separate channels for my loop and click-volume levels.

Here is how I wire my system for live use. This particular Mini-disc Recorder has two sets of outputs:
1. Left and right XLR outputs and,
2. Left and right RCA outputs.
Therefore I send the RCA left and right to channels 1 and 2 of my line mixer (Figure 2), and I send the XLR left output to the House P.A. system (Figure 3). (I do not send the right channel to the House P.A., because I do not want them to have the click track.)

 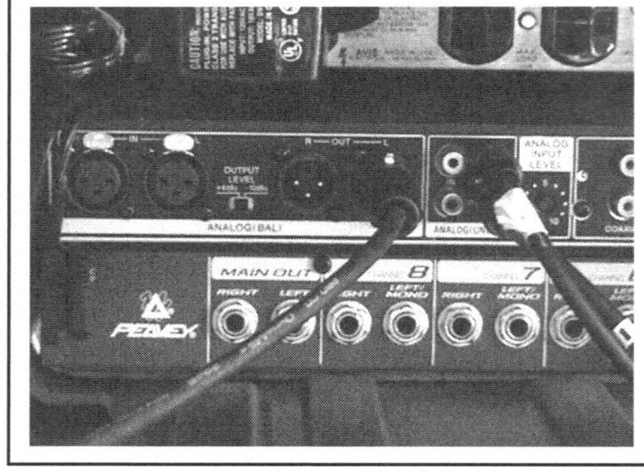

Figure 2

Figure 3

Thus, when I press play on my Mini Disc Deck it sends the left-loop channel to the P.A. through the Left XLR output, and it sends both the left and right RCA outputs to the line mixer. Therefore, I can adjust the volume level of the click and loops in my headphones independently of the signal that is being sent to the House P.A. **This configuration is my most advantageous setup.**

Figure 4: A Portable Travel Solution

Every now and then, I am not able to bring the four-space rack case on the road. Thus, I have this small setup that fits into a small "carry-on" bag as well. This setup contains the following items (counterclockwise from the top):

- **Surge Protector** (and multi-outlet extension cord). This is a standard item that can be found at any hardware store. It provides power to all my separate portable devices and it protects them from power surges.
- **4-Channel Compact Desk Mixer.** The mixer acts as my own personal headphone-monitoring system with separate channels for my loop and click levels.
- **Portable Mini Disc Recorder.** This item provides the loops and backing tracks. (The loops are recorded to the left channel and the click is recorded to the right channel).
- **DI Box.** This item converts an unbalanced audio signal to a balanced audio (XLR Cable) output signal.

The wiring in this scenario is identical to the previous example with two exceptions:

1. This portable Min -disc Recorder only has one headphone output. Therefore, I use a stereo Y- cable (Figure 5: one 1/8" stereo cable to two mono 1/4" cables) to split the left (loop) and right (click) channels of the headphone output into separate signals. Then I connect it to channels 1 and 2 in the desk mixer (Figure 6).

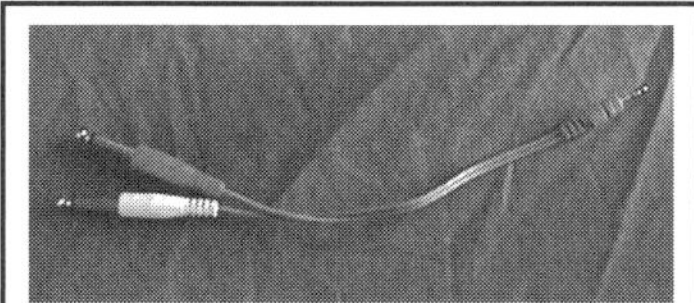

Figure 5

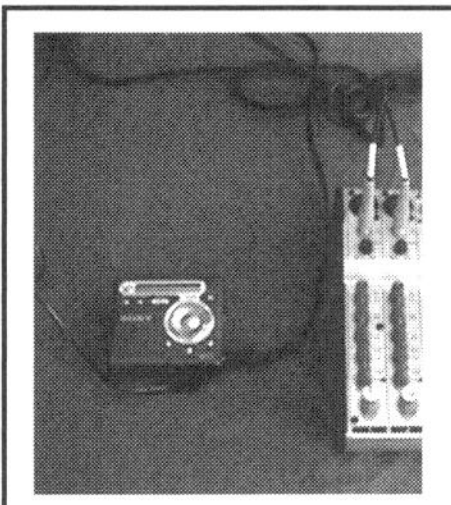

Figure 6

2. I connect one mono cable from the left (loop) output of the desk mixer into a DI box. I then attach the DI box to an XLR cable which is used to send the balanced audio signal to the House P.A. (Figure 7). **Remember:** I do not send the right channel to the House P.A. because I do not want them to have the click track.

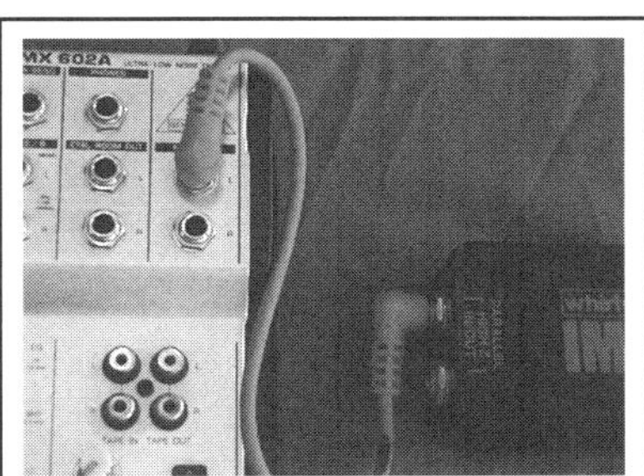

Figure 7

Altogether, the wiring for the portable setup looks like this (Figure 8).

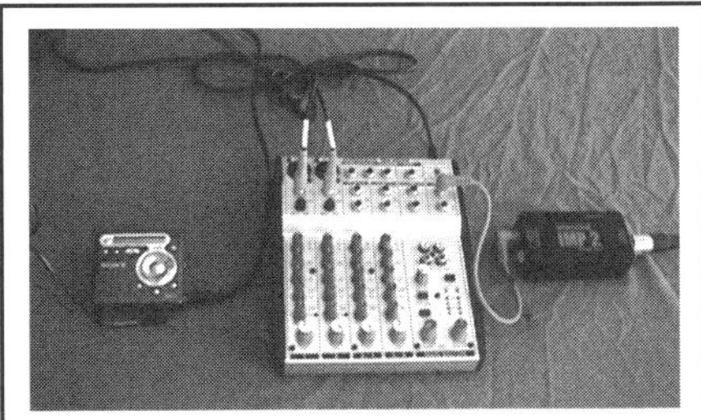

Figure 8

However, this setup does have a disadvantage: Because this portable mini-disc only has one headphone output, I cannot change my personal headphone volume on the desk mixer without changing the House P.A.'s volume as well.

Setup 2: A Mini-disc Recorder, Headphones, Line Mixer, Laptop and Drum Kat (for Manually Triggering Loops and Loop Fragments Live)

Figure 9

As I stated earlier, I use the Rackmount Mini-disc setup for most of my loop and backing track-based performances. However, there are occasions where an artist's material (or performance process) requires me to alter the length of each song's Verse or Chorus to fit a particular performance. In this situation, I augment my Rackmount Mini-disc setup with a laptop and MIDI controller. This arrangement allows me either to: (1) perform with the Mini-disc Recorder or; (2) manually trigger loops live (and in real time) and monitor them all through my line mixer.

So in addition to the Rackmount Mini-disc Gear, I have added the following equipment:
- **Apple G4 Powerbook loaded with Ableton Live and Propellerheads Reason Software.** These items provide all of the loops, samples and backing tracks.
- **Alternate Mode Drum Kat.** The MIDI controller that converts my stick hit(s) into MIDI information.
- **M-Audio 1x1 USB MIDI Interface.** This item allows my laptop to communicate with the Drum Kat.
- **DI Box.** Converts an unbalanced audio signal to a balanced audio (XLR Cable) output signal.

Here is how I wire my computer system for live use:
1. I connect a Y-cable (one 1/8" stereo cable to two mono 1/4" cables) from the headphone-out of my Powerbook into channels 3 and 4 of my eight-channel line mixer (Figure 10):

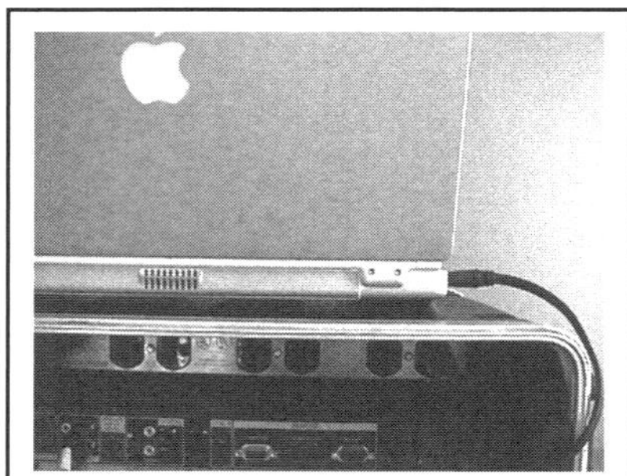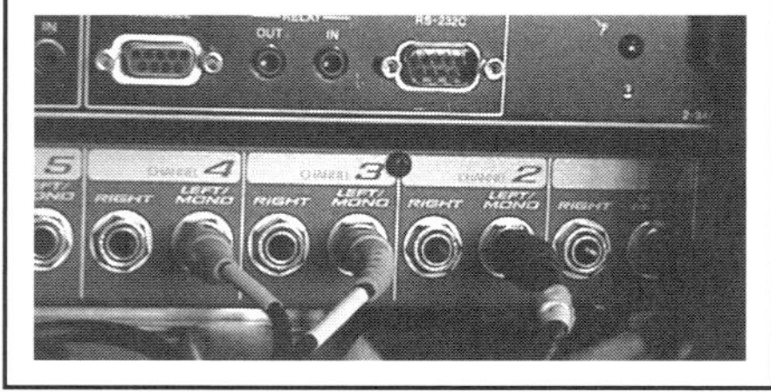

Figure 10

2. I connect the MIDI In and MIDI Out of the M-Audio USB MIDI Interface to the MIDI Out and MIDI In of the Drum Kat (Figure 11).

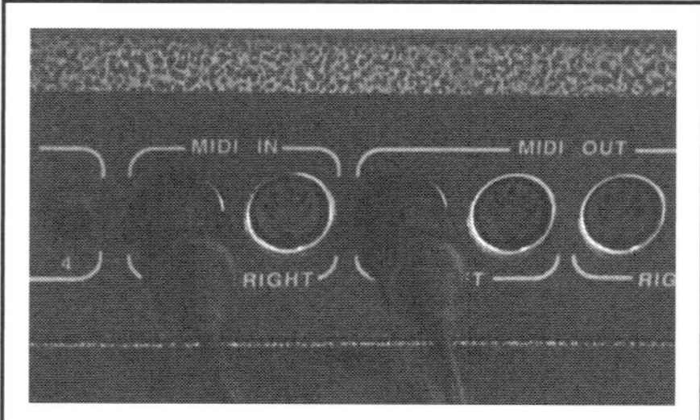

Figure 11

3. Then, I connect the USB Portion of the M-Audio Interface into the USB Port on my Powerbook (Figure 12).

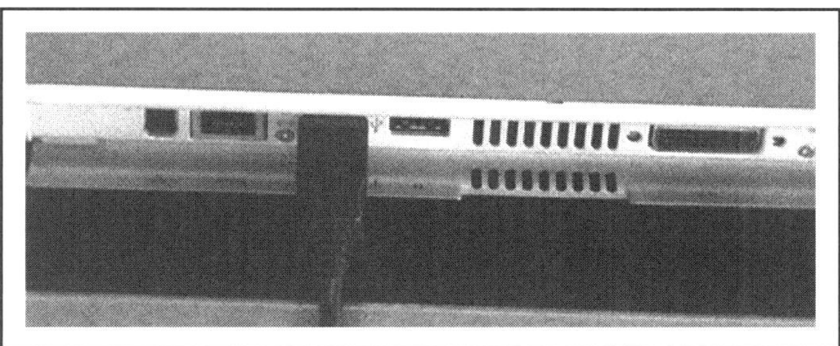

Figure 12

4. Finally, I connect the output of my line mixer into a DI Box, which connects to an XLR Cable (Figure 13). This cable is used to send the audio to the House P.A.

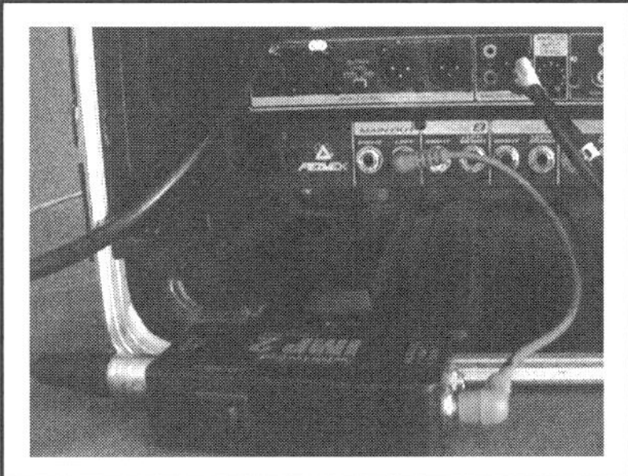

Figure 13

Thus, when I strike a pad on my Drum Kat, MIDI information is sent to my laptop (and software), which in turn translates that MIDI information into audio. Secondly, that audio is routed out of my laptop's headphone output and then sent into channels 3 and 4 in my line mixer. Thirdly, (and almost immediately) that audio is sent to my line mixer's output, which is connected to the DI Box. Finally, the DI Box converts the audio to a balanced XLR signal, which is sent to the House P.A.

Important Note: Since the audio signals are now all routed through my line mixer, I cannot change my personal headphone volume on the line mixer without changing the House P.A.'s volume as well.

Setup 3: A Laptop and Drum Kit (for triggering various samples and sound FX that are "not timed")

Figure 14

When I perform with an artist that only needs a few drum, percussion or Sound FX samples triggered in a show, I use the computer gear from Setup Three (without the Mini-disc Rig).

Here is how I wire this computer system for live use:

1. I connect a Y-cable (one 1/8" stereo cable to two mono _" cables) from the headphone out of my Powerbook into two separate DI Boxes (Figure 15).

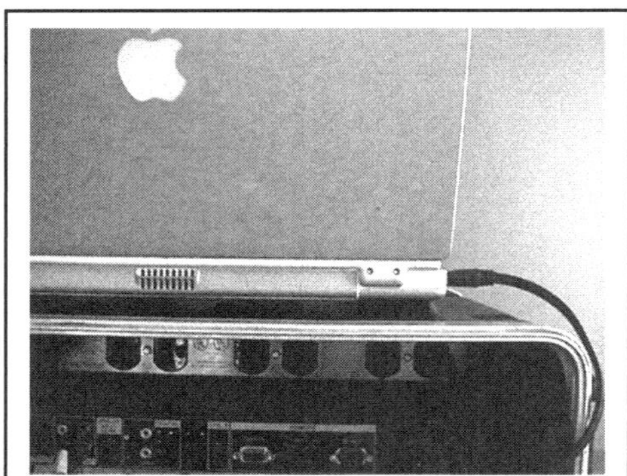
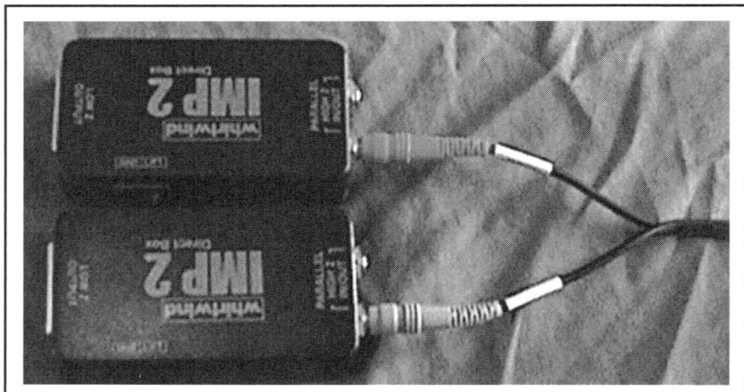

Figure 15

2. I then attach an XLR Cable to each DI Box and send them to the House P.A (Figure 16).

Figure 16

Important Note: Since I am not performing to "timed" elements, I will not require a click track (or need to monitor these sounds in any way.) Therefore, I do not need a line mixer in this situation.

Setup 4: Adding Acoustic Drum Triggering

Figure 17

In addition to all the previous Setups, I am occasionally required to trigger drum samples from my acoustic drums as well. (This is done to fatten up the acoustic drum sound with specific drum samples that are integral to an artist's song). Therefore, I add a Ddrum 4SE Module (Figure 18) and triggers to my live rig as well.

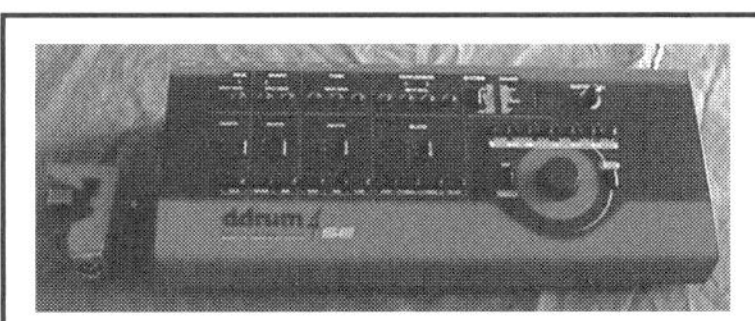

Figure 18

The Ddrum Module is very useful because I can load it with custom samples and trigger them from my drum kit. Furthermore, it is specifically designed to trigger from acoustic drums. (Most samplers are equipped to trigger from keyboards or electronic pads. Thus, they are not designed to handle the vibrations that are generated from acoustic-drum playing.)

Here is how I wire my Ddrum Module for live use:
1. I fasten a trigger to my bass drum, snare drum and three toms.
2. I connect the cables from each trigger into the Ddrum Module. For example, the bass drum trigger is connected to the Kick (bass drum) input on the module (Figure 19).

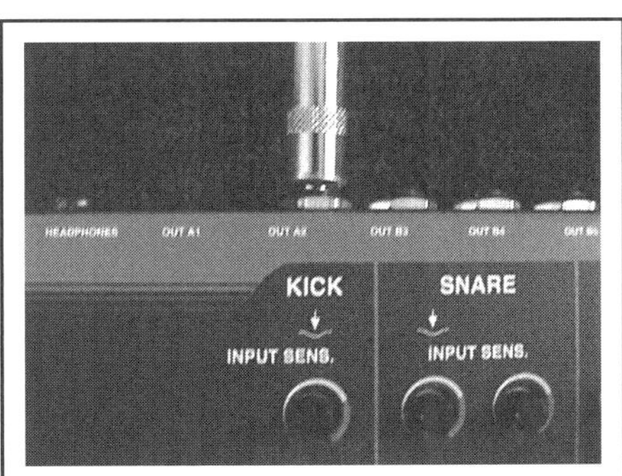

Figure 19

3. I then connect the left and right audio outputs of the Ddrum Module with _" mono cables into inputs 5 and 6 in my line mixer (Figure 20).

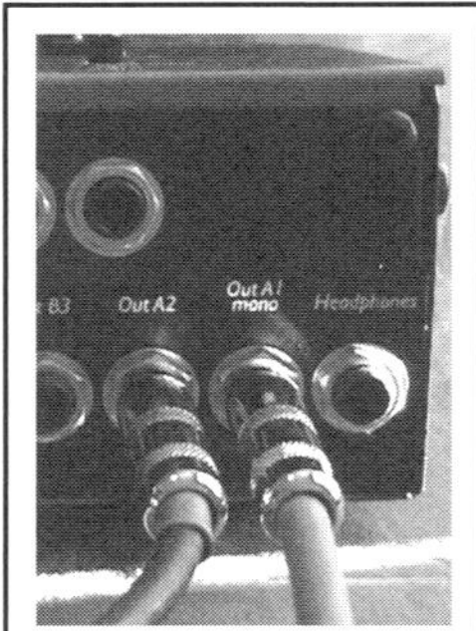
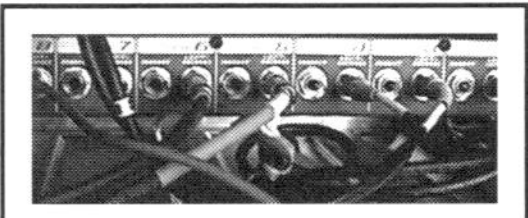

Figure 20

4. Output of my Line Mixer into a DI Box to send to the House P.A (Figure 21).

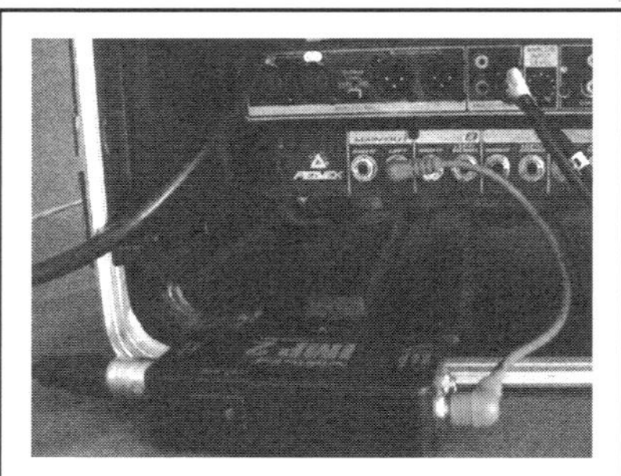

Figure 21

Thus, when I strike an acoustic drum, an electric current is sent to the Ddrum Module, which in turn translates that information into audio (drum samples). Then that audio is sent from the Ddrum Module to channels 5 and 6 in my line mixer. It is subsequently "mixed" with all the other audio signals from the Mini-Disc and laptop and then sent to the line mixer's left output. Finally, that left mixer output (which is connected to the DI Box and converted to a Balanced XLR signal) is sent to the House P.A.

Thus, with all of the devices connected to my line mixer, the rear input section of the line mixer looks like this (Figure 22):

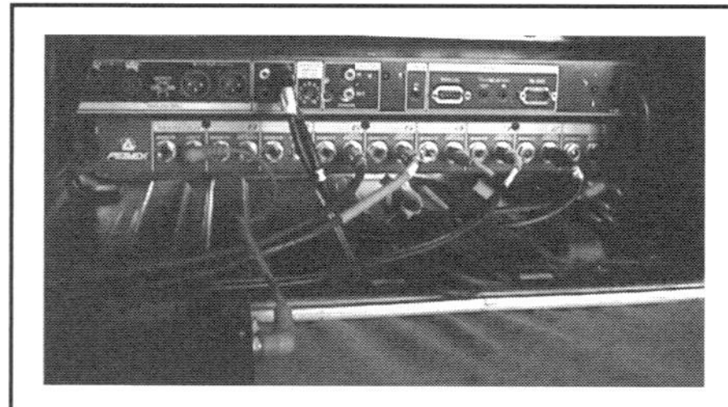

Figure 22

A Final Word on Electronic Setups

Please keep in mind that these electronic setups are not all-inclusive. They are illustrated in this section to serve as an entrance point into the world of creating your own custom electronic rig. Furthermore, I do realize that I mention two brands (Ddrum and Drum Kat) quite frequently in this section (which I believe are best suited for my professional needs). However, there are many other suitable brands of electronic devices on the market as well. I encourage you to do your own homework before purchasing any particular item.

Appendix E: Software and Its Concepts

The Basics

In order to program tracks effectively, it is very important to understand four concepts:

1. **MIDI vs. Digital Audio.** MIDI is an acronym for "Musical Instrument Digital Interface." This technology allows many different instruments to communicate with one another. MIDI does not record or deal with audio in any way. It merely records a series of numbers that deal with issues like note type, velocity, duration and timing. Each issue has a value from 0–127.

2. **Digital Audio Workstation (DAW).** Digital Audio is different than MIDI in one very important way. Whereas MIDI deals with numbers that correspond to musical performances, digital audio actually records musical performances like a traditional tape machine, but on the computer platform. Here is a simple DAW (Figure 23):

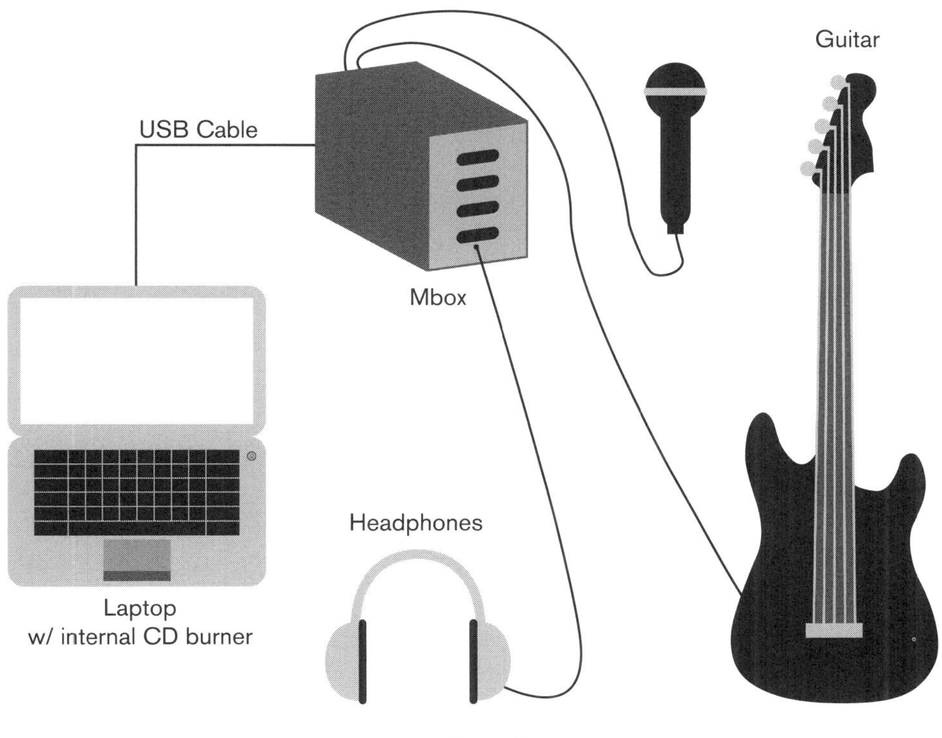

Figure 23

A MIDI keyboard can also be hooked into this setup via USB as well.

3. **Software Synths.** They are synthesizers, samplers and/or drum machines in software (rather than hardware) form.

4. **Plug-Ins.** Software Synths that plug into your main DAW or MIDI Sequencing Software. (They show up in the main program as one channel on the mixing board.)

Software
The main software programs that I deal with are all standards in the Recording and production industry:

- **Pro Tools (DAW).** Records digital audio and has limited MIDI capabilities as well.
- **Apple's Logic Pro (DAW).** Records digital audio and has advanced MIDI capabilities as well.
- **Ableton Live (DAW and MIDI).** Records digital audio, stretches loops to any tempo and has MIDI capabilities as well.
- **Propellerheads Reason** (MIDI Sequencing and Soft Synth). Has MIDI capabilities and provides all the Software Synths and samplers in a virtual rack of gear.
- **Spectrasonic's Stylus (Plug-In).** Provides a drum sample and loop playback engine (as a plug-in) within Pro tools.

Functions of Each Piece of Software

Master Program (Pro Tools and Logic Pro). The Master Program records all of the audio in the studio such as guitars, drums and vocals. After the initial recording it also controls all tempos, editing, mixing, location and MIDI functions.

Slave Program (Reason and/or Ableton Live). The Slave Program follows all the commands of the Master Program. However, the Slave still fulfills its requirements, such as providing sounds and FX devices.

Plug-Ins. These are essentially Slave Programs, but they open within the Master Program. This means that they are part of the Master DAW file and not a separate file and program too. Thus, they are more user- friendly because you only save one file: the Master File. (They too follow all the master program's instructions as well.)

Important Technology Note: Please keep in mind that computer-based music is evolving at an extremely fast rate and since software is ever-changing, many of the terms presented in the previous paragraphs will be outdated in a few years. Consequently, these concepts are an entrance point into computer music, and they should be utilized to help you develop an initial vocabulary (and conceptual understanding) on the matter.

These are the basic concepts needed to implement and utilize electronics into your drumming repertoire. Remember, using these techniques in conjunction with acoustic playing can be an extremely adventurous and rewarding experience. After working with these effective loop/sample methods on a daily basis, not only will your workflow improve, but your new programming skills will grow exponentially. As always, immerse yourself in this new world and enjoy it.

In addition, please study this material diligently and be patient. Look to famous drummers who use some of these approaches, read magazines, surf related websites, and talk to individuals who are already knowledgeable in these matters

Websites and Additional Reading

All around information:
Tweakheadz.com. Website that covers all topics that relate to computer and hardware music-making.

ComputerMusic.co.uk. The computer-music-magazine website that covers all major issues about making music on a computer. It has reviews, articles, and tutorials for Mac-and Windows-based machines.

Hardware-based samplers and sequencers:
Akaipro.com – Akai Musical Instruments (check out the MPC series of combo sampler/sequencers; they are usually perfect for drummers.)

MPC-tutor.com. Tutorial and info site specifically for Akai MPC combo sampler/sequencer machines. Offers tutorials on loop making, sampling, beat chopping and drum programming.

Software-based samplers and sequencers:
M-Audio.com. Company website that is devoted to developing hardware and software products that make music on computers (home systems and laptops).

Propellerheads.se. A software company that creates loop-chopping software, sound-creation software and even drum-machine emulation software. Check out the products titled: "Recycle, Rebirth, and Reason."

Ableton.com. Designers of Ableton Live 4.0 Sequencing/Looping software.

Digidesign.com. Developers of the Pro Tools Recording Platform.

Apple.com. Makers of the Powerbook Laptop Computer and Logic Pro DAW.

Trigger interface pads etc.
Alternatemode.com. Company that makes the Drum Kat and other various trigger pads, pedals and MIDI interfaces. The most advanced and sophisticated midi-controllers for Drummers.

Clavia.se. Makers of the DDrum Electronic Drum Triggering System.

Appendix F: The Real World

Main Gig Scenario
When I am called upon to play with an artist that augments their stage performance with backing tracks, loops and samples, I receive two things prior to a rehearsal or performance: 1) The full tracks on CD(s) that have been released, and 2) A CD, Pro Tools Session or Mini Disc of all of the prerecorded backing loops.

Here is an example of how I usually develop my parts when I perform with a prerecorded backing loop/track:

Gig Preparation
1. I listen to the fully completed song(s) from the artist's CD and I make some detailed notes (and charts) on what grooves and tones are present in the mix. For example, I notate the exact grooves (and percussion parts), the song's form (Verse, Chorus, Bridge etc.) and other subtle ideas such as "a lot of low tones present in the song; play high voices on the Kit."
2. Secondly, I then listen to the backing loops/track by itself to see if the form on the track is the same as the CD. In addition, I listen for what parts are being played by the backing loops/track. Again, I make many detailed notes and charts.
3. After that, I compare both sets of notes side by side. I then look at what parts are missing from the backing loops (or what parts need to be reinforced), and those are items (or grooves) that I play on my drum kit.
4. Lastly, at rehearsal (if there is one), I make sure that the artist (or musical director) likes my artistic choices and drum parts prior to the performance.

Appendix G: Supplemental Texts

If you need any additional information on basic drumset technique, reading or other related issues, I suggest that you examine one of the fine instructional books listed below.

Texts That Relate to this Book
Patterns Volume 3: Time Functioning Patterns by Gary Chaffee.
This is a great book for drumset reading, creativity and independence. It contains linear playing, Jazz patterns, Rock & Funk patterns and *Harmonic Coordination*.

Studio & Big Band Drumming by Steve Houghton.
Although, Big Band is in the title of the book, this text is really about chart reading in all styles of music. Therefore, it is a must for any drummer.

Some of My Favorites (in all Styles and subjects)
The Art of Bop Drumming by John Riley.
A wonderful all around study on Jazz drumming (and music). It deals with Jazz timekeeping, soloing, and basic brush techniques.

Practical Applications of Afro-Cuban Rhythms by Chuck Silverman.
This text is great entrance point into the world of Afro-Cuban music, rhythms and drumset independence. A must-have!

Practical Play-Along by Chuck Silverman.
A supplemental play-along package to the previously mentioned practical-applications book.

The Drummer's Complete Vocabulary as taught by Alan Dawson by John Ramsay.
I studied the "Alan Dawson Methods" during my studies at Berklee. These are the concepts and techniques that have really stuck with me over the years! Thus, this book is wonderful for developing your reading skills, independence, application of rudiments and conceptual knowledge on the drumset.

It's About Time by Fred Dinkins.
This is a wonderful study on time and groove playing. Fred has many detailed exercises on how to play in the middle, ahead and behind the Beat.

TAKE IT TO THE NEXT LEVEL!

AKIRA JIMBO

Fujiyama – Combining Acoustic and Electronic Drums - Book w/ CD (DRM108)
Fujiyama (DVD7)

Wasabi – Adding Spice to Your Groove - Book w/CD (DRM107)
Wasabi (DVD1)

In *Fujiyama*, Akira reveals his concepts on the use of acoustic and electronic drums and how they can be integrated into a unique playing style. Major topics of discussion include location of trigger pickups, trigger function modes and programming drum patterns. *Wasabi* helps drummers add spice to their groove and tells of his personal journey into the discovery of his drumming personality. DVDs are in English, Spanish and Japanese.

DAVE WECKL

Exercises for Natural Playing - Book w/CD (DRM110)

How to Develop Technique (DVD8)
How to Practice (DVD9)

In *How to Develop Technique*, Weckl explains his natural approach to the drums in clear language and with careful demonstrations. In this DVD, he focuses on wrist technique, stick grip, finger technique and the rebound approach to both hands and feet. *How to Practice* centers on hand and foot development, independent practice, Swiss triplets and his own warm-ups. In *Exercises for Natural Playing*, Weckl offers the reader exciting new exercises and concepts not covered in the DVDs including insight into hand positioning, the Moeller technique, bass drum pedal work, time and motion and playing without losing time. DVDs are in English, Spanish and Japanese.

STANTON MOORE

❖ **Rated 5 stars by Modern Drummer** ❖

Take It To The Street - Book w/ CD (DRM115)
A Study in New Orleans Street Beats and Second-line Rhythms As Applied to Funk

A Traditional Approach to New Orleans Drumming (DVD15)
A Modern Approach to New Orleans Drumming (DVD16)

Mix it up New Orleans Style and *Take It To The Street!* in this comprehensive book and two DVDs by one of the Crescent City's hottest drummers. In this series, Stanton focuses on street beats, funk, clave and second-line drumming along with his personal insight into becoming a truly gifted and musical drummer.

RICK LATHAM

Advanced Funk Studies - Book w/2 CDs (RLP1)
Contemporary Drumset Techniques - Book w/4 CDs (RLP2)

Advanced Funk Studies 25th Anniversary (DVD18)

Drummers have considered Latham's best selling books *Advanced Funk Studies*, which Modern Drummer calls one of the 25 greatest drum books ever published, and *Contemporary Drumset Techniques* as 'must have' publications for decades. Latham also celebrates 25 years with this Anniversary DVD that includes material from both books focusing on linear playing and includes exclusive interviews legendary drummers Ed Shaughnessy and Louie Bellson.

These publications are available at your local print music dealer.

For more information about Carl Fischer Music log on to:
www.carlfischer.com